LINDA

Linda Perfect lives in Kent in the t a
lifetime studying and working with ual
Life Coach, Psychic Advisor, Poet ad
more about her work at www.magi follow her on Facebook
at Linda Perfect- Magical Life.

First published by Linda Perfect 2012
Second edition published by Odd One Out Publisihing 2015

002

Text copyright © Linda Perfect 2012
Linda Perfect has asserted her right under the Copyright, Design and Patents Act 1988 to be identifed as the author of this work

This book is sold subject to the condition that it shall not, by way of trade or otherwise, be lent, resold, hired out, or otherwise circulated without the publisher's prior consent in any form of binding or cover other than that in which it is published and without a similar condition, including this condition, being imposed on the subsequent purchaser.

ISBN-10: 1478396121
ISBN-13: 978-1478396123

www.oddoneoutweb.com

Typeset by Odd One Out Publishing

LINDA PERFECT

THE STORYTELLERS TAROT

ODD ONE OUT
PUBLISHING

CONTENTS

Prologue   7

Chapter One: Tarot and Story   13
Chapter Two: Therapeutic Uses of
Tarot and Story   31
Chapter Three: Story Teaches Tarot   39
Chapter Four: Tarot Teaches Story   49

Major Acana Stories   61
Minor Acana Stories   157

The End   251
Epilogue   253

PROLOGUE

Tarot is...

Tarot is alive, organic spiritual, and full of magic this living language speaks to me of multi layered mystery.

Tarot tells it like it is in rich symbolic images of patterns in the energy the more I look the more I see.

Like all good books this one has a beginning, middle and an end. The real beginning goes back half a lifetime to when I discovered the Tarot and began an endlessly fascinating journey of discovery. Like most who are drawn to work with the Tarot my initial interest was in divination. In those far off days it was not so easy to obtain information about the Tarot, books and packs of cards were not available as readily as they are today. However, I was persistent and searched out many books on my solitary quest for knowledge. Some of the books were helpful, others too obscure and complicated. As I struggled with these learned tomes the Tarot itself evolved beyond the older packs that had been available and one year, for my birthday, I was given a pack of cards that were themed by the Arthurian stories. Here I made a great leap in understanding, by seeing the Magician represented as Merlin, I understood much more about what the card was showing me. The familiar King Arthur was much easier for me to relate to than the stony faced Emperor in the old fashioned cards. I began to explore myths and legends and over the coming years was easily able to link them to the Tarot as many more themed packs became available. I had, during this time become accomplished in divination and regularly gave consultations to clients where I often found myself referring to well-known myths and legends to explain a card to a client. In doing this I rediscovered my childhood love of stories. Many times in my life I had identified with the characters in the books I read. As I delved deeper into the realms of story I found not only was I identifying parts of myself, but seeing the archetypes and characters of the Tarot that figure in my life and those of my clients as well. Doing this gave me a much broader and deeper understanding of the Tarot. It also brought to my attention how both Tarot and story had the potential to heal, teach and inspire and for the two to work in combination would be doubly empowering.

Combining these two is not an entirely new idea; one of the first known uses of Tarot was for storytelling as entertainment. As early as the sixteenth century tarot cards were used for inspiration for poems written by court ladies in Italy. There are also excellent examples available today , of stories written by modern authors using Tarot as their inspiration, that entwine ancient knowledge with modern day, or even futuristic , viewpoints. These stories give us a glimpse of the potential of the Tarot; like stories old and new it has the power to inspire, to teach and to bring about transformation and healing.

The Tarot is as flexible as a dancer and the beginning of the book explores how it works with many different types of story by identifying cards with characters and the events of the plot. The myth, legend and faery tales I have used as examples in Chapter one demonstrate how the wisdom of the ancient tales can be revealed again with the help of the Tarot. The wealth of Tarot packs available now facilitates ready-made links to the inherent wisdom of the myths legends and folk tales of many different cultures.

But it is not only ancient stories that can be explored through the Tarot. The same archetypes that people those myths and legends appear in different guises with different names in the stories on our bookshelves today and can also be identified with the cards in the Tarot pack. It is quite easy to identify the Tarot in sci fi and fantasy fiction, much of which relates to the old mythic themes, but all categories of modern stories can be included here. The stories of our modern culture are as important and relevant to our lives as were the ancient myths and can teach us as much about ourselves and our lives. Again, using the Tarot to grasp the underlying meaning of a story has the dual purpose of also giving a deeper understanding of the Tarot and showing that its energy is accessible in modern day situations as well.

One of my own first encounters with a magical character from relatively modern times was Mary Poppins, who's mysterious like I did not meet again until I recognised her in the magical and mysterious Tarot High Priestess. Both had magical knowledge that was a closely guarded secret- Mary Poppins carpet bag was as mysterious as the book the Priestess holds on her lap. Mary's everyday clothes were even similar to the dark blue robes adorning most representations of the High Priestess. Mary knew, as intuitively as the High Priestess, exactly where she was needed most and with the elusive quality of this card disappeared again when her task was done and those she had been with had learned what she had to teach them.

I wondered as I mused on this, if Shakespeare had written his play "The Merchant of Venice" with the Justice card to inspire him as the play tells of a higher power than Shylock that weighs, not a pound of flesh, but the truth of a heart. The Devil too, was easy to identify in John Updike's "Witches of Eastwick" as the character who led the three women on a merry dance creating illusion after illusion…

Neither is the Tarot's relevance limited to fiction, true stories too can be seen in the cards , after all our own lives are not fiction and fantasy but fact, whether it is the true story of a famous person or of a client with an ordinary life having a consultation.

But I discovered that Tarot and story can be used for other purposes too. Chapter two discusses the therapeutic uses of Tarot and Story, giving examples and case studies that apply the theory to all kinds of problem solving. I have found in my own work with clients that the therapeutic value of story combines well with the healing power of the Tarot. The lesson or problem a client needs to understand and that can be clearly seen in a Tarot card, can be explained with a story, often more familiar to a client that the image on the card that they may not have seen before. A story relating to a card can also provide a client with the guidance they need in a form that is easy to understand and remember.

The middle of the book explores how writing stories can be therapeutic as well as helping to develop creativity. It is not necessary to be a Tarot expert to use the cards to inspire stories. I have found the Tarot a rich and limitless source of inspiration for poetry and stories and would definitely prescribe it as a cure for writer's block! Chapters three and four give exercises for individuals and groups to make stories for healing and for spiritual development as well as for inspiration and entertainment.

This brings me to the final part of the book; the Storyteller's Tarot itself, which consists of seventy eight original stories. One story for each card.

These stories are my personal interpretations of the energy of each card based partially on my twenty years' experience of studying and working with the Tarot, and my study of story. I say partially because the stories were not written or planned in the normal way a writer would approach writing a story. I had reached a stage in my work with the Tarot that went beyond divination to a more creative and flexible use. The Tarot had demonstrated many times to me over the years its excellent ability to provide guidance so I began the task of writing the stories by choosing a card at random thus allowing the Tarot itself to steer me through this journey. Although the stories appear in traditional order in the book to avoid confusion, they were not written in sequence. The cards seemed to tell me their stories when they saw fit, switching me from major to minor and from element to element. This may be a suggestion from the Spirit of the Tarot for the reader to do the same and select stories to read at random rather than in order.

I have provided no other interpretation for the cards than the story, but have left the reader to find their own magical key to the card within the story. Each reader responds to a story from their own personal perspective and the meanings of the cards need to be personally experienced to be truly understood

The purpose of my stories is to stimulate a deeper awareness of the underlying power of the message contained in each card and to demonstrate its relevance to our own life experiences.

The End discusses the conclusions that can be drawn from this exploration into the combined use of Tarot and story and how these conclusions can be applied in today's world.

As an Epilogue I have included a unique Table of Correspondences that enables the reader to relate the cards to all different kinds of character and of story, both ancient and modern.

I have constructed this Table from my own bookshelves and my own memory, including as many different kinds of stories as possible, but it is merely an example. I would like to encourage readers to choose their own correspondences from the stories they know and love and that are relevant to their own view of the cards.

CHAPTER ONE: TAROT AND STORY

Many different types of stories work well with the Tarot. This chapter will show you how stories, that are widely available to anyone, can be related to the Tarot.

MYTHS

One of the types of stories most told is myth. Myths are stories that come from the misty region between memory and dream. In ancient, pre literate times these stories were taken to be true accounts that explained human history, behaviour and development. The themes and characters in myths often embodied ideas, religious beliefs and the meanings behind social customs and value systems.

Ancestral wisdom and lore was also passed down through the telling of these stories, often in the form of the feats of seemingly super human beings. This wisdom and lore was more likely to be remembered if imparted in the form of a story that could be told and re told. Most ancient cultures had interlocking sets of stories, rituals and customs that gave the people a meaning and direction to their lives giving them both security and a sense of identity.

The Age of Reason and Science cut mankind off for a long while, from this deep rooted knowledge, dismissing myth, magic and even Nature herself as unimportant, cutting the collective unconscious off from its imagination and spiritual self. But myths are not merely tales of bygone ages and their value is far deeper than just historical curiosity. Recent times have seen a great revival of the ancient hero myths in the very modern, space age, tales such as Star Wars. Modern people follow the mythic journey on Star Trek. These stories strike chords in our own memories as the journeys and dramas of our own lives unfold. The actual origins of Tarot are wreathed in myth and it too, has been dismissed as merely a card game or fortune telling device. But the archetypes of the Tarot relate directly to, and are common to, all mythologies, as they do to the stories of our lives. The ancient mythic heroes, the Tarot Fool and ordinary people like us are all traveling on a journey through life.

Many Tarot packs use a particular mythic theme to help explain the cards. You can now buy Tarot relating to Egyptian, Greek, Native American and Celtic myths, to name but a few.

Because myth and Tarot relate so closely it is possible to re tell a myth with the aid of the cards.

The Celtic Myth of Taliesin could be told as a simple story with these cards; The Goddess Ceridwen - with the knowledge of the High Priestess, has made a magic brew, mixing and combining the ingredients for knowledge and inspiration, like the traditional Temperance image, in a huge cauldron. But her brew must simmer for a year and a day without boiling over or spilling one drop. So she hires a little boy called Gwion, as innocent as the Fool and an old man called Morda, as old and wise as the Hermit. At first things go well, the boy and the old man become friends, affection flows between them like the two of water, and the task they are given seems to be an easy one. But then disaster strikes, maybe the two friends drifted into complacency, maybe not. But the cauldron boiled over, the burning liquid splashed on Gwion's thumb and without thinking, as instinctively as the Moon, he sucked it- two things happened simultaneously-it was if the lightning struck Tower exploded burning and scarring the land with destruction, Gwion too was as if lightning struck him, instantly he was illuminated and had full knowledge of the World.

With this bright knowledge came the fear of the Devil like anger with which the Goddess would pursue him. Fearing her wild Chariot would run him down Gwion began to shift shape as the chase began, using the transformative energy of the pages of earth, water, fire and air to flee her as a hare, a bird and a fish, finally coming to rest on earth as a grain of wheat.

But the Goddess swallows him and holds him in her womb for nine months, like the nine of cups then, as the Empress, becomes his mother. As mothers does she let her child go, but in a leather bag- a container like the ace of cups-she casts him into the fast flowing river- like the river of Death that divides this world and the other.

But the story is not over yet, for this miraculous child is called, like the summoning at Judgment, to be rescued from the river and reborn once again as Taliesin, called Radiant Brow because he glows like the Sun, who has the gifts of poetry and prophecy from the cauldron of inspiration and the womb of the Goddess- transformed from the simple childish Fool, to the wise Hierophant, the guardian of tradition.

This is not the end of Taliesin's story, and the brief telling above could be expanded and fleshed out further. However, initially, simple telling's of myths were best remembered. The story of how Gwion became Taliesin is a story of transformation. The cards I chose to tell this story show that transformation, simply and clearly.

This is not the only myth that could be told with the cards either; any myth from any culture could be re told in this way- for pure entertainment or to understand the myth and the cards on a deeper level.

LEGEND

A legend is a popular story handed down from earlier times whose truth has not been ascertained, although there usually is some kernel of truth to tempt the reader to believe. One such as this is the legend of Thomas the Rhymer, who did actually live in Scotland in the 13th century. It is not Thomas's life that is the subject of legend, but his death. Some versions of this tale say that he accurately predicted his own murder and others say he was carried off to faery land to serve for seven years. Another legendary figure is Robin Hood, said by history to be the Earl of Huntingdon, whose fight against oppression inspired stories that have been handed down for hundreds of years. One of the most famous British legends is that of Arthur, the Once and Future King, who will return when he is most needed. Like myths, these ageless and inspiring legends can be traced and re told using the Tarot.

The Legend of King Arthur could be told as a story by the following cards. First we see him as the Fool, the innocent, who has no idea what lies ahead of him. He hopes and expects to become a knight like his brother Cei, just an ordinary knight of earth, a humble soldier following orders. But the Wheel of Fortune has a greater destiny in store for this young man, pulling a sword from a stone-literally the ace of swords- changes his life. Like the Hanged Man, his life is turned upside down and his whole perspective is altered, any personal hopes he may have had are sacrificed for the hopes of the people. He takes up arms to establish law and order and becomes the Emperor, with the power and responsibility for ruling. With Guinevere, his Empress he rules the land for many years, with Strength and Justice, until at last his time is done and he faces surrender to the ten of swords- Death in battle. He is born away to Avalon by the High Priestess

Morgan and her nine sisters to the Moon's dreaming realms to sleep and heal. But the Star of hope still shines, for Arthur will return, when Judgment calls him forth to the daylight world of the Sun, to be King again.

I have skipped through a simple version of the story- but this could be explored on a much deeper level, using many more cards, to examine the various challenges Arthur faced and the events and relationships of his life. A wealth of books tells the many stories attached to the mass of Arthurian legend. The cards I have selected could also be explored on a much deeper level too; writing more than the sentence or two I have used for each card would make the story fuller and richer. You could, for instance explore the deeper significance of Arthur's personal self being sacrificed for the good of the land, and how this links with the underlying meaning of the Hanged Man. The Wheel of Fortune card could also refer to the famed Round Table, giving a multitude of story possibilities. The Ace of cups, a card I have not even touched on in my version, could tell the story of the Holy Grail, of healing and inspiration, sought by the Arthurian knights.

There are several Tarot packs on the market with Arthurian themes and those relating to many other legends that would be a great help for students wishing to explore this.

FAIRY TALES

Fairy tales, of enchanted princesses, wicked stepmothers and mythical and magical beings are often of traditional origin and told mainly to children. The hidden magical elements in these tales seem to continue to work long past childhood, and it is possible to access a deeper meaning in many of them. They differ from myths and legends in that it is rarely claimed that they are true, unless you are one, like me, who believes in faery tales. This statement is not as crazy as it sounds because the same archetypes of the Tarot that are common to myths and legends are also present in fairy tales as kings and queens, magicians and witches or heroes and villains, where they also tell of the experiences we face as we travel through life, and not all of them have happy endings. The jealousy of the wicked stepmother is something many people experience, so is feeling like poor down trodden Cinderella. A more pleasant example is the awakening of Sleeping Beauty, maybe not always by a kiss from a handsome prince but in many shapes and forms. The longing for a happy ending and to be the beautiful princess leads many to plan faery tale weddings.

In his book The Magical World of Tarot, Gareth Knight asks us to imagine that Cinderella comes to consult the Tarot. He then tells her story using a structured Tarot spread that could apply to anyone in similar circumstances- demonstrating how fairy tales relate to tarot and how both relate to our own lives. I have used a less structured method to use the cards to tell the story of; The Goose Girl, just choosing one card for each character and event in the story.

I begin with the Queen of air, traditionally a card used to portray a widow, in this case the mother of our heroine. She is a princess betrothed to a prince in a far of kingdom whom she has never met. The Moon describes her feelings and her situation- she is to leave her dear mother for the first time in her life, she feels mixed up and confused, maybe full of fear of the unknown, but she instinctively knows that it is right for her to take this step, and part of her dreams of becoming a queen in her own right. The ten of earth shows the wealthy dowry the Queen prepares for her daughter, included in this is a maidservant for the princess. The maidservant turns out to be the villain of this particular story with some of the qualities of the page of air; she is jealous, malicious and spiteful. The Queen of air gives two magical gifts to her daughter before she leaves on her journey. The first is white handkerchief with three drops of her blood on it to help her daughter when she is in need, this gift relates to the 3 of air, a card of understanding and transforming sorrow. The second gift was a horse that, according to the Brothers Grimm, was called Falada.

Falada was no ordinary horse as she could speak and like the 7 of water would eventually reveal both truth and illusion and thus save the princess.

The journey begins badly, the maid refuses to get a drink from the stream for the princess and as she leans down to get a drink for herself the handkerchief her mother has given her falls into the water and floats away, leaving her weak and helpless. Now the princess feels the sadness of the 5 of water. The wicked maidservant takes this chance to force the Wheel of Fortune to cast the princess down to a lowly maid and herself to wear the robes and ride the magical horse of the Queen's daughter. She is determined that she and not the princess will marry the king's son. She forces the true princess to take an oath that she will not reveal the treachery; entrapping her like the 8 of air can prevent free movement.

Both the King and his son, like the King and Knight of earth, believe what they see and the maidservant, using the cunning of the 7 of air, succeeds in her plan to convince them she is the true bride. The princess is given the job of accompanying the page of earth like little boy who tends the geese. The false princess entreats her new fiancé to summon the knacker to destroy Falada, claiming that the horse was troublesome on the journey but really intending to prevent the horse from speaking of what she had done. So like the ten of swords, Falada was under sentence of death, but the goose girl who had once been a princess heard of this and promised a gold coin to the knacker if he will nail Falada's head to the archway she takes the geese through. This, like the Ace of earth, is the beginning of truth manifesting. For every morning as she passes through Falada speaks to her of how sad her dear mother would be if she were to know what had happened.

The goose boy tells the king of these strange conversations and one morning the king hides behind the arch to listen. That evening he sent for the goose girl and asked her why she spoke thus to the horse's head. The oath that she had taken would not allow her to tell him so he sent her to the Tower and told her to tell the truth to the walls. Relieved that she could at last release the truth, as the tarot Tower shows us, the goose girl poured out the whole story. The king now sees the truth with the clarity of the ace of air and realises he must take action.

With the sense of purpose of the Ace of air, he plans a wedding feast, like that often depicted by the 4 of fire. The true princess is seated, dressed in glorious finery, to one side of the prince and the deceitful maidservant sits on the other side, not noticing her former mistress. As the feast ends the king challenges the maidservant to solve a riddle, with the cunning of the Devil, master of deceit, he tricks her into pronouncing punishment for her own crimes. From her own wicked mouth she is condemn to be trapped inside a barrel and dragged through the streets by a two horse Chariot until Death claims her. The Wheel has turned again and the prince and princess are then left to marry and enjoy a 10 of water style happy ever after.

This is a story of truths and illusions, which the cards illustrate very clearly, with the deceits shown by the 7 of air and the Devil and the truths revealed by the Ace of air and the Tower. Truth and illusion in our own life can be explored using these cards; what would you have whispered to the Tower's walls? The page of air jealousy that motivated the maidservant could also provide much food for thought, especially as the punishment she eventually suffered was so drastic. The way the Wheel of Fortune regained control over the situation and righted it teaches us to have faith in rightness and truth, no matter how bad things seem. Another question to consider could be why the princess, like so many of us, had to suffer the dark night of the soul the Moon card takes us through before she found her happy ending.

The magical gifts that the princess receives also resonate with our lives. Have you ever received a gift that helped you in an unexpected way o when you couldn't help yourself, like the goose girl? The source of the princess's gifts was her mother; you could trace and explore the source of your own gifts using the cards to help you.

Other faery tales too, contain deeper meanings that we can help to reveal by using a corresponding tarot card. Rachel Pollack, in her book Forest of Souls, discusses the story of Rapunzel, another story in which the Tower has a prominent role to play

You can use any Tarot deck to tell faery stories, there are now many to choose from. A good example of this is The Inner Child deck; the authors have made use of many traditional faery tales that link perfectly to the wisdom of the tarot.

CLASSIC AND MODERN FICTION AND TAROT

It is not only ancient tales that have something to teach us. Classic and modern fiction continues the tradition in the same vein. Characters in the books we read now and the life situations they face are sometimes easier to identify with than those of a legendary figure or magical being. Some characters and their experiences can also be related back to the archetypal events and mythic heroes of our ancestors. As well as identifying with the characters in the stories we read, we can also study the deeper meanings of the story and how they can help us in our own lives, using the Tarot.

WUTHERING HEIGHTS

The passionate tale of Wuthering Heights is a classic love story that can be easily told with the cards. This story could have the Wheel of Fortune as its introduction and theme card- for it is Mr Earnshaw's fateful action of taking in to his home the wild and brooding Heathcliff- who the book tells us could personify the Devil- that changes the fate of his family and of his home. Wuthering Heights weathers the storms depicted in the Tower card many times in this story. At first we do not realise what the consequences of Mr Earnshaw's action will be as Heathcliff and Catherine Earnshaw, the daughter of the house, are drawn together like the soul mates of the Lovers card, and grow up together on the wild and lonely moors.

The Wheel turns when Catherine decides she will marry Edgar Linton. The King of Water could play the role of Edgar- a gentle, courtly young man, with delicate health- totally opposite to robust, uncouth Heathcliff. Heathcliff's hopes of marrying Catherine are dashed and again he is made to feel as outcast as the five of earth when he overhears a conversation about her intentions between Catherine and Ellen Dean, her nurse and narrator of the story. This character is confided in by all of the others, playing a more passive but vital background role similar to that of the High Priestess. Heathcliff disappears- deciding like the 8 of water, to move on, as nothing remains for him here if Catherine is to belong to another.

So, like the two of water Catherine and Edgar are united in marriage and all is well until Heathcliff returns. Neither he nor Catherine can forget each other or their lives at Wuthering Heights, which does not sit well with Edgar. It seems for a while that Heathcliff controls the Wheel- for it is through gambling that he forces Catherine's brother to relinquish Wuthering Heights to him in payment of a gambling debt-riding over him roughshod like the warrior in the Chariot card. It seems the fortunes of the Earnshaw's are sinking and like the Emperor, Heathcliff takes control of their lives and begins to implement his vengeful plans. In spite he marries Edgar Linton's sister Isabella, who finds that like the 7 of water, her vision of him is an illusion. The truth of Heathcliff's cruel ways hurts poor Isabella like the 3 of air and she flees, bringing up her baby son as far away from Heathcliff as she can.

Then the Death card takes over the story as Catherine dies giving birth to her daughter- Heathcliff, still furiously jealous of Edgar and passionate about Catherine, howls his grief at the Moon. But Death plays into his hands when Isabella too dies and his own child is returned to him. A child he intends to use as a puppet in his schemes. As he plans, Catherine's daughter and namesake, who is a lively minded protective child like the page of air, eventually meets his son, her cousin Linton, a weak and selfish page of water. Ellen Dean reveals to the reader Heathcliff's plan for the two young people to marry. Using the wit and cunning of the 7 of air, he is able to gain control of Edgar Linton's lands and property as well as Wuthering Heights. Edgar is now very weak and ill and near to Death, when Heathcliff imprisons Mrs Dean and young Catherine at Wuthering Heights until she weds his son. But young Catherine finds no happiness in her marriage and the deaths of both her father and Linton leave her at the cruel mercy of Heathcliff, who now controls all that belonged to her family- it seems he has now risen to the top of the Wheel and she to the bottom. As Heathcliff's plans all slot into place Ellen Dean reveals to us the haunted life he has led-like the 9 of air his mourning for Catherine torments him and as time passes grows stronger. It is while he is lost in his longing for her that young Catherine becomes close to her cousin Hareton- the true heir to Wuthering Heights who still lives there. Hareton, like the knight of earth, has worked for Heathcliff all of his life and is rough and uneducated, though under his roughness lies a much kinder heart, one that can love even Heathcliff. Heathcliff's grief progresses from the 9 of air to the 10. He surrenders to death to join Catherine at last in her moorland grave. But this is not the end of the tale. Like the 10 of air so often shows- a new beginning will come from it, as Ellen Dean tells us of the ace of water love that has grown between Catherine and Hareton, who will be married on New Year's Day. Here we find that the Wheel has turned full circle and Wuthering Heights has been returned to the Earnshaw family at last.

Although the Wheel of Fortune dominates the story as a theme, the other major cards have a lot to tell us about the deeper aspects of this tale. The Lovers and the Devil are, by tradition, opposites. These two cards give us a clear picture of the conflict the story is built around- a love that is tormented. There is a great and lasting love between Catherine and Heathcliff. But when Catherine chooses to marry Edgar the Devil's influence shadows that love, because Heathcliff thinks he has been betrayed and this culminates in his plans to take control of all the properties of the Earnshaw and Linton families in revenge for his loss of Catherine. Is it because relationships are so difficult, and we all fight devils in the name of love, that this story has never lost its appeal? Many of us fight to gain control of our anger in some way. In the story the Chariot, which often indicates a form of defence of our inner feelings, the Emperor, who likes to be in control, and the explosive Tower all come into play, as Heathcliff seeks to destroy those he sees as his tormentors and take control of their possessions. It seems the Devil has turned love to hate.

The influence of the Moon and Death cards add to the passion in the story at the climax when Catherine dies bearing a daughter and Heathcliff howls his grief at the night. Heathcliff's grief manifests in cruelty and viciousness. How many of us turn nasty and spiteful when we face rejection and loss and go through the dark night of the soul the Moon can indicate?

The end of the story can only come when the Wheel has turned full circle and Heathcliff too dies. For only by surrendering all that he has gained and allowing it to return to those it rightfully belongs to, can he be reunited with his beloved Catherine. Although our own romantic affairs may not be so dramatic the ending of the story shows how the turning of the Wheel can restore the balance of life and love and it is by surrendering control that happiness is found.

Many stories can be enjoyed and learned from in this way;

REBECCA

Daphne du maurier's Rebecca is a story of another love triangle- this time two women - the unnamed narrator of the story and Rebecca, the late wife of the central male character Maxim de Winter. It is easy to align Tarot archetypes with the two women. Rebecca and her successor are as different as chalk and cheese- or as the High Priestess and the Empress. Rebecca fits into the Empress role- with her renowned physical beauty, attractive, it seems, to all who meet her and an impressive chatelaine for the fabled Cornish home of the De Winter's- Manderly. Manderly could be depicted by the ten of earth- a card of domesticity that sometimes shows a mysterious stranger outside the gates.

The second wife is as opposite to Rebecca as she could possibly be, she says she is plain and gauche, passive and lacking in confidence. She has a hint of Cinderella about her; unlike flamboyant Rebecca she has no money, no family and no real friends. She may have believed Maxim de Winter to be her Prince Charming when she came upon while working as a companion to a rich American. She suppresses her emotions and is insecure and secretive- much more of a High Priestess, with her womanly potential hidden beneath plain clothes. The fact that we never know her Christian name adds to her mystery, again linking her to the mysterious High Priestess. The strange little happening she mentions also relate her to this card; that she had bought a postcard of Manderly long before she met it's owner; that she begins her tale with the recounting of what turned out to be a prophetic dream about the destruction of the house.

The differences between the two women become more marked as we get into the story- one is dead and one alive (but both play equal roles in the story), one is named often and the other nameless, one is assertive and the other almost totally passive, and Rebecca, although she is dead, seems indestructible as her successor becomes more and more mentally and emotionally fragile.

Maxim de Winter is a character that would fit the Hermit in the Tarot. He is a mature man in his early forties whose first experience of marriage has caused him to withdraw into himself- at first, like our heroine, we are led to believe he has gone abroad to get away from the scene of a beloved wife's death, but Maxim hides a secret.

The main them card for this story could be the Lovers -it is a story of relationships- how the heroine imagines Maxim's relationship with Rebecca, the relationship she herself is developing with him. The opposite of the Lovers- the Devil, comes into play here, for not only is our heroine under a complete illusion about Maxim and Rebecca's marriage, her own relationship with him is marred not only by the rivalry with a dead woman, but by the shameful secret Maxim is hiding from her.

On their return to Manderly she attempts the impossible task of filling Rebecca's shoes, not helped by the spiteful Mrs Danvers, who could be described as the Queen of air at her worst. Before long she begins to obsess about Rebecca, as despairing as the 9 of air of ever coming out from under her shadow she begins to feel haunted. Maxim is cold and distant, leaving her to sink into depression, she begins to endow Rebecca with all the qualities she feels she lacks- again the Lovers and the Devil entwine themselves in the story.

The next cards turned are the Tower and Death when at last the true facts of Rebecca's death are revealed.

Surprisingly our heroine sustains her High Priestess passivity and accepts Maxim's story completely and stands by fervently hoping that the truth will remain concealed. Her fears, which could be illustrated by the tarot Moon, manifest in a second dream in which she and Rebecca combine to destroy Maxim.

A surprising twist puts Maxim in the clear by indicating a motive for suicide but the Tower destroys Manderly, the house of secrets, like fire, and the de Winter's are forced into lonely exile abroad.

Although a sad and haunting tale there is much we can learn here. The clearly contrasting characters of the two wives show very different aspects of womanhood as do the images of the related cards- an interesting question for a woman would be; which of these two would you most identify with? and for a man; which would you be attracted to? The clarity with which Du Maurier drew these characters shows how deeply she must have considered the different characteristics. Both the wives of Maxim de Winter have more negative characteristics than positive, giving us a glimpse of the shadow side of both of these cards.

The image of opposites is a constantly recurring theme in this book illustrated by the Empress and High Priestess, Lovers and the Devil, the 10 of earth and the Tower. We can see how truth and illusion can become indistinguishable, confusing our relationships and causing the havoc and destruction we read of in this story.

Changing relationships, similar to the second wife in the story, are more common today than ever and many people consult the Tarot to try to understand their feelings and cope with the problems that arise in their situation. The Lovers and the Devil, High Priestess and Empress are often cards that feature in the answers offered by the Tarot to this type of question. Countless writers have written stories using different types of male and female characters, using the contrast between an active dynamic man who could be compared to the Tarot Magician, and a strong but silent character, like the Tarot Hermit.

The Mayor of Caster Bridge by Thomas Hardy could have the Hanged Man as a theme card, to show how Mike Henchard takes an oath to give up drink for twenty-one years. Many times through life we have to sacrifice a personal desire to attain a higher good. Nicholas Evans' book The Horse Whisperer could have the Strength card to illustrate its theme, for the hero uses gentleness and love to strengthen and heal an injured horse. This book has much to teach us about Strength, what it is and how it needs to be used in a balanced way and tempered with gentleness.

Edward Rutherford's epic novel The Forest could have the tarot World as its theme card. It describes the 'world' of the New Forest containing all elements of life within itself.

The list of stories that can be liked to the cards is probably endless, so I will leave you to find more examples on your own bookshelves.

What significance does this have for us as students of the tarot?

My personal experience of combining the use of Tarot and Story has shown me that this way of working can yield far more than ordinary advice anyone might expect from the Tarot and teach far more than a story alone would. Making the connection between the energy of the card and that of a story helps us find to the deeper messages contained in both as we go beyond the painted image to touch the energy it represents and that we illustrate with the story. (This can been taken further by finding several stories that relate to one card, widening even more the possibility for interpretation.) This in turn reconnects us to our roots, to the times when our ancestors received wisdom and guidance from mythological sources in particular. The accumulated folk wisdom of many cultures, as sources to help us understand our psychology and spirituality, are again becoming popular and have as much relevance to our lives as stories and as Tarot cards created in modern times.

CHAPTER TWO: THERAPEUTIC USES OF TAROT AND STORY

FACING SHADOWS

All heroes or heroines have to face an adversary at some point in their story. The stories of our lives also contain dark aspects of life and of us. It is often very helpful to accept and learn to work with these dark aspects for they have much to teach us. Both Tarot and story are ideal tools for this sometimes daunting task. In the story of Peter Pan, Peter had to have his shadow sewn back on by Wendy as he was incomplete without it, as the Tarot would be incomplete without the shadowy Devil, which demonstrates clearly for us two points; the first being that darkness and shadow are as much a part of life as light and clarity, the second being that you are never alone in facing your shadows as everyone has them, we always cast a shadow. Shadows and darkness can be used very creatively; the popularity of books with these themes, like the classic Dr Jekyll and Mr Hyde and the modern tale on the same lines by Steven King "The Dark Half", to name but two, demonstrates this well. Both authors have explored the 'evil twin' or shadow side of their heroes. Shadows are by nature mysterious and difficult to pin down but they do not always manifest as dramatically as evil twins. Our shadow self may manifest as depression, anxiety, or the more destructive addictive or obsessive behaviours. Most of us do not like our shadow aspect and we often try to deny the existence of the part of us that behaves badly, maybe lies, cheats or betrays.

Sometimes we are not aware of the shape of the shadow in our self and just have an unidentified feeling of unhappiness blocking our progress. The Tarot can be used to identify and work with the shadows in our lives, using this, as a focus for a therapeutic Tarot consultation can be very helpful. The Tarot itself makes this an easy way to understand the darkness, as every card has a negative as well as a positive, each containing light and dark aspects. The Sun may appear the brightest of cards but it also contains the negative point that too much of its heat may burn, or the truth that it clarifies may hurt. The Devil can be seen as an image of fear that can feel threatening and challenging, but whose positive lesson offers us the opportunity to find the courage rise to his challenge and release ourselves from his domination.

One of the best ways of working with shadow aspects is to try to learn to use them creatively. It is possible to consult the Tarot to identify shadows within the self.

This can be done by asking the Tarot to show an image of your shadow and then randomly selecting your card, or by consciously choosing an image from the deck that represents your shadow for you. The next step is to work with the images through writing or telling a story, working through the shadows and using the dark images to heal (some people prefer to use reversed cards for this process although personally I find this confusing) and thus shedding light upon them and creating a shift in the energy that has been blocked.

A client of mine selected the Death card as an image representing her shadow. The blockage to her personal progress that this card represented was her fear of change and inability to let go of parts of her life that were no longer necessary. The related story work that followed was an effort to change her perception of 'death' by removing the fear. To demonstrate the positive aspects of major changes I used the story of Sleeping Beauty. Her death was magically averted but in consequence, she and all those in her world stayed asleep and unaware of life for a hundred years. I asked my client to imagine nothing moving or changing in her life and the stagnation that this would result in. Then finally the prince removes the spell from Sleeping Beauty with a kiss and she awakens once more.

This happy ending shows my client the positive aspects of major change as we discuss how excited and happy Sleeping Beauty must be to wake to life and all its possibilities.

Another client who had help from a faery tale was a lady who felt very much like Cinderella; put upon and abused as if her life were nothing but drudgery. The initial card she selected was the Moon. Discussion of this story identified her need to find her own inner faery Godmother, in order to transform her situation as Cinderella was transformed to go to the ball. The card she selected to help her with this was the beautiful Empress, a card that expresses loving and nurturing energy my client needed.

Both parties knowing the story, as in the two examples given above, created a link between client and therapist and some good fertile common ground for communication. The simple images and symbols in stories can relate very directly to what is going on in the client's life.

The exaggerated quality of the symbols in faery stories, illustrated by the Tarot cards selected, can make the problem much clearer, and using both tarot and story as a source of metaphor, enable the client to identify their problem clearly and become more objective about the issues they need to address.

It is not always necessary to use a complete story, any image, theme or motif may be used on its own, sometimes only a brief reference to a well-known tale is needed to interpret the theme the card is pointing out to the client. An example of this is the reference to the well-known legend of Arthur pulling the sword from the stone to reveal himself as the true king to explain the quality of truth expressed by the ace of swords.

Bringing an oral telling of a story into the therapy session in this way connects us to the ancient and primal art of communicating wisdom through storytelling and restores the humanity to the therapy session, helping the client to feel much more comfortable and to gain the trust in the therapist that is necessary for healing to take place.

In another instance of the combination of Tarot and Story in a therapy session I used the story I had written about the Fool to demonstrate to the client the adventurous and carefree attitude he needed to take to make the most of a career opportunity he was being offered, rather than let his shadowy fear of failure hold him back.

HEALING

The purpose of my work as a Tarot therapist has always been to try and make my clients feel better. The following account describes how Tarot and Story combined to show me a way of providing some real healing. I had developed a new service for my clients. I arranged for the client to select some cards, from which I wrote them a unique personalised story. Being able to produce these stories attractively, thanks to the computer, also made them a suitable gift for clients to give friends and family. A regular client of mine, who I shall call Jane, commissioned a story for her friend Lisa's birthday. She chose nine cards at random while focusing her thoughts on Lisa. As we laid the cards out my eyes were drawn to the Tower, while Jane picked up the ten of cups.

"I like that one" she said, "It looks like 'happy ever after', that's what I'd like to give Lisa for her birthday". "Happy ever after" became the title of the story before I had written a word.

As I began work on the story it became clear that the Tower was the theme card. An ancient story of warring dragons beneath a tower in the time of Merlin came to mind as I studied the card. I knew from experience that even in story form the Tarot would have a message to impart and it was clear to me that these warring dragons had some significance. So I wove a modern tale of how the conflict of the dragons was resolved.

The story had an unexpectantly potent effect on Lisa and related directly to a tragic part of her life. The spirits trapped beneath my fictional tower represented Lisa's grief for twin sons who had died shortly after birth several years before. This grief had been trapped inside her for a long time and she had never found a way to confront it. The story triggered a release of this grief and seemed to have an on-going healing effect as Lisa opened her heart to her family and friends and they were able to begin to find their way to the happy ever after the story ended with.

But this story turned out to have a second chapter where Lisa had a second story that she wanted to read for her two little sons when she visited their grave, written from cards she chose herself. As I sat to write this story it struck me that most children like to hear stories about themselves and Lisa's two little boys became the heroes of a story called The Magic Star. This story was by far the easiest I have ever written- and I have written many stories with and without the cards. It was as if the two small boys in my story sat either side of me dictating the whole thing. It became as much of a tale to tell their mother, as one for her to read to them. It was quite an uncanny experience, but a very real and touching one.

This simple children's story brought not only some degree of explanation, but also a marvellous amount of comfort to Lisa and her family. It enabled her to connect with her lost children in a very real way. Those around her reaped the benefit to the degree of Jane saying she had become a new woman.

We all relate on some level to stories; they are a safe and familiar format. There is a clear example of this in the use of storytelling to help the 9/11 trauma victims being documented as highly effective.

This beautiful and moving experience brought me to the conclusion that Tarot and Story combined can bring about a profound healing. With a client willing to trust in the process this method could be therapeutic in dealing with many other painful issues in a gentle, non-threatening way.

DREAMWORK

Everybody dreams, and often dreams contain messages and information that is very helpful to us, if only we can access it. Dream, Tarot and Story form a magical triad that enable us to do this. The analysis of dreams is an art as old as story, with roots more ancient than the Tarot. The way to begin analysing a dream is by studying the images and events in it, which are often symbolic, as are the images depicted in the Tarot. The main link between dreams and Tarot is that both are symbolic languages, bringing information to our consciousness via images with underlying meanings. In both too, there are many levels and layers of meaning, but it is possible to see clearly and understand our outer lives, as we see them reflected in the mirror of our dreams or mirrored in the cards. The dreaming state connects us with another level of reality that can also be accessed through the Tarot.

Each dream has a story that can be made sense of through an analysis of its scenes and images. Dream symbols can be very obscure but it is possible to explain them by translating them into Tarot to get a clearer sense of their meaning. Relating the Tarot symbols to the story then completes the magical triad.

A client of mine was having disturbing dreams. Over a period of time we began a series of Tarot sessions aimed at unravelling and finding the meaning inherent in these dreams and discovering their relevance to her outer life. After several sessions we found ourselves focused on a particular card that I had just used as a theme card for a story. The story had a similar setting to a key dream in the series my client had had and, along with the theme card, became the key that unlocked what her dreams were telling her. This enabled work to begin directly on the underlying issue we had discovered in order to begin to restore her normally healthy patterns of sleep and dreams.

These are just some of the ways Tarot and Story can be used therapeutically. I have found it particularly helpful when the client is very sensitive and when what they are dealing with is very painful for them. This kind of therapy is gentle and non-threatening and helps the client to cope with difficult issues in an easier way.

CHAPTER THREE: STORY TEACHES TAROT

Combining Tarot and Story has proved to be a very useful tool for teaching students about the Tarot. Stories are ideal to illustrate the energies depicted on the cards and their likely influences. Using stories inspired by the cards and stories known and loved by all, a deeper understanding can be facilitated.

TEACHING INDIVIDUALS

Two very different students of the Tarot demonstrated two things to me very clearly; the usefulness of the Storyteller's Tarot as a proven teaching tool and how stories we all know and love can also be used to understand the Tarot and ourselves.

The student I will call Alice is a young woman in her mid-twenties. She is a beginner with the Tarot although she is very sensitive and has a very natural ability to work with the cards. I like to tailor the lessons I give to the individual student and this student is a very artistic and imaginative person. I knew her to be a very conscientious student but did not want her enthusiasm to become bogged down in boring lists of possible meanings and influences. I wanted to bring the cards to life for her. So instead of referring her to the classic Tarot text books and their lists I told her original stories and poems, illustrating each card with either or both to give her a real feeling for the card that she could relate to.

This worked like magic - her response was far better than I had expected. She grasped the essential quality and energy of the card quickly, by relating it to these quite simple tales. She picked out from the stories a considerable amount of information about the card and wrote about her own understanding of the story and what she learned about the card from the story. She commented how magical it was and how it was much easier to remember a card when she could link it to the story. When, like all Tarot students do, she came across a card that she found difficult to understand, I used the story I had written for the card to explain what she had been unable to grasp from looking at the image. After only a short while, she paid me the ultimate compliment of asking for a copy of the complete set of my stories when she had read only a few. Her learning was supplemented by other kinds of study, but the stories were the heart of it. She read many stories and ' normal' Tarot textbooks, by many writers, that gave her many different views and kept her flexible in her use of the cards rather than getting locked into a list of set meanings.

Another student; Barbara is a very different person to Alice. She is in her forties and has been learning about Tarot for several years. It was a consultation on a feminine health issue arising in her life that led us to begin a study of two particular cards that relate to femininity; the High Priestess and the Empress. To illustrate these archetypes we related them to the two wives of Maxim de Winter in Daphne du Maurier's Rebecca. Barbara was an avid reader with an interest in classic books.

She had never read Rebecca before or realised that the Tarot could relate to a story in this way, or that it could actually help her. This work really stimulated her.

She thoroughly enjoyed the book and asked me to recommend another. She was able to clearly see the qualities of these two cards in du Maurier's characters and how several other cards also related to the story and could be used to tell it, like reading the plot from a Tarot spread. She also identified how qualities of both these cards appeared in both women, as they combine in all women and how these qualities manifest in her. This gave her a deeper understanding of her own femininity and helped her to nurture herself and thus improve her health in a rounded way.

A second instance of Barbara making a break through using stories was with the Court cards. Like many people, Barbara found the Court cards quite difficult to interpret and had got stuck with a vague physical description of a person the card may represent with an equally vague astrological reference. So Barbara and I entered a period of studying the court cards, singly at first. For each Court card chosen, usually at random, I gave Barbara an original story I had written relating to the card, that she read and we then discussed it. This work was very fruitful as Barbara began to see that there was much more than a 'person' in each of the cards.

She realised that there were circumstances and events, and sometimes more than one character, in the stories that related to the card's meaning or the type of energy it represented. She began to get a much better feel for the Court cards from the stories, by understanding the actions, feelings and characteristics of the people in them; she began to be able to identify how many ways the Court can relate to herself and her own life. The stories seemed to enliven and animate the still figures on the cards so Barbara could more clearly interpret their significance in a spread. We then identified characters in other stories from our bookshelves that could relate to the Court cards, giving Barbara a wider perspective of them.

Once we had got to know the stories of all the Court cards we began to discuss how this or that character would relate to another. What would the Queen of water have to say to the Knight of air? What do the four Queens have in common? This too proved quite fascinating and the blockage that Barbara had had about these cards really began to disappear - she came to feel more at ease with them.

Both students gained much new understanding by identifying which elements of the stories related to particular symbols depicted on the cards to illustrate their underlying energies. From using a diverse selection of stories they also learned how diverse the interpretation of a card could be, without losing the basic underlying meaning.

When working with these women with my own original stories, both of them saw things in the stories that I had not consciously put in them, but which were nevertheless, very much there. This added to my own knowledge, making this a learning experience for all concerned.

All of the work done with Tarot and Story combinations was fruitful and helpful and deepened all of our understanding of the Tarot.

TEACHING GROUPS

The Storyteller's Tarot can also be used for teaching groups of students. I came to realise this when one of the major arcana stories I had written was read out loud to a group. When asked for comments I noticed that the group members had all picked out differing aspects of the story, all relating to the card. The resulting discussion became a sharing of information as everyone's views on the story and its symbols and images were heard. This gave all the students a wider understanding of the energy of the card and what it was likely to convey in a Tarot consultation.

There are many ways groups of students can learn more about Tarot through storytelling. A group of six or seven people can have one card each to make a group story, where each member's contribution is based on the card they hold. This is an entertaining way of learning more about the cards and gaining the benefit of the contributions from the rest of the group as well. Another way of working would be to give the group one major card to focus on and make their story from their combined input on the single card. A third variety is to give six people the same card, let each make a story on their own, then come together afterwards and compare the six stories. Four small groups can each be assigned one of the minor arcana suits from which to construct their story. You can be as inventive as you like.

On one occasion I wrote a story, focusing on the group of people who had planned a Tarot study session as I selected cards at random from which to build the story. This story was to serve three purposes. The first was entertainment, to share a story is always entertaining, whatever its source. The second was recognition of the influences of the cards used in the story, leading to a fruitful discussion on the influences and the interaction between them. The third purpose was to offer the group a challenge; to make their own story from the same cards - not necessarily in the same order or with the same theme. This last exercise served not only to demonstrate the versatility of the Tarot but also of the group members.

CHAPTER FOUR: TAROT TEACHES STORY

The combination of Tarot and Story can also be used to help the development of creativity and storytelling. Tarot cards are the ideal ' story triggers ' and can be used to develop the twin skills of Tarot interpretation and storytelling. There are lots of ways in which the cards can be used to inspire and write or tell a story.

ONE CARD METHODS

Using just one card is the ideal way to start. Any card in the pack can be used in several ways. One way to try is to select a card, sit quietly with it, studying the image and then use what comes to mind as a story theme, loosely basing a story around the basic theme of the card. For instance; imagine the major Justice card has been selected, this card opens up an array of options for a story: giving rise to the questions; who seeks justice? For what and why? This could be a story about a court case or the righting of a wrong done in a personal conflict. It could be a story of karmic justice and could be set in any time period you want it to be. The symbols on the card can also be brought into the story and help to stimulate events in the plot, the scales of justice are often seen outside courtrooms and Shakespeare's Shylock weighed his pound of flesh on a set of scales.

Minor cards are equally suitable for this kind of storytelling. And in the same way the story can be triggered by symbols on the card. I once wrote a story using the Ace of earth. The Tarot pack I was working with showed an image of a ring as a symbol for the Ace of earth and my story began with a woman finding a ring. You could also use the general theme of a card as your story theme. In the example below I used the theme of the ten of fire for my story. Ten is the last of the numbered fire cards and the vibrant energy of the suit is now much reduced - sometimes burnt out. Like all tens it signifies an ending of some kind in a person's life that allows for a new beginning; which gave me the idea for Ash.

ASH

Ash was shattered, tired out and exhausted. She had fled the city in a panic, burning up the miles in her fancy sports car until all the hassle; the hangers on and flunkies were miles behind her. She was finished with fame - ten years at the top was enough. She stared at herself in the mirror; the harsh light of the cheap motel room did her no favours. Flame red hair that had to be dyed every few weeks to cover the gray threading through it, crow's feet around the notorious emerald eyes and the blurred jawline that would become a saggy old woman's neck. She had had it- her face had been her fortune and that of all the users and abusers as well - now she was finished - burnt out and old - used up and spent. She laughed bitterly - what would they do when the golden goose stopped laying eggs for them?

When the vibrant flame could no longer illuminate a stage or captivate an audience? She was too tired to care. She pulled back the bed covers - one night's sleep would not be enough. She wanted to go into hibernation - buried deep somewhere and then slowly fade into obscurity until she disappeared entirely in a puff of smoke.

Early the following morning Ash sat hunched over a table in the fast food restaurant, smoking a cigarette and drinking strong coffee, hoping no one would look her way. The restaurant was almost empty and the bleary-eyed night shift waitresses ignored her. She was still tired; she had slept heavily but was not refreshed. She didn't have the strength to get up and move. She didn't even have any plans, or the energy to make any.

A discarded magazine lay on the uncleared table in front of her. Idly, she turned its pages as she smoked her cigarette. She reached the horoscope page, and from force of habit that she was unable to resist she looked for her sign; Sagittarius. "Time to reinvent yourself" she read, and a tiny spark came to life somewhere within.....

A year later and fifty miles down the road from the motel; two women stood talking about a third in the post office-come-supermarket in the village of Little Oak.

"She reminds me of someone, I just can't think who" said the milkman's wife.

"That's Miss Ashton from Phoenix House," answered the postmistress, as the subject of their curiosity closed the shop door behind her. "She's a bit of a recluse, someone said she writes children's books, but I don't know if it's true or not."

Ash smiled as she walked up the street, running a hand through her silver hair. She was thoroughly enjoying her new role. How well it suited her!

METHODS WITH MORE THAN ONE CARD

You can increase the scope of your story by using a group of cards. A good way to start is to select three cards at random from your pack and lay them in a line to represent the beginning, middle and end of your story or as you could try seeing them as your two main characters and the conflict between them. You can, if you wish use the three cards in any order you like to shape your story. The possibilities are almost endless.

As you gain more experience of using more than one card you can build it up to more, though I would recommend keeping it at less than ten. Again, you can use the cards in order of appearance or any other order you choose. You can choose your cards at random from the deck or you can make your own choices (I personally find random choices work better). You can also assign 'roles' to your cards; such as 'theme card',' main character card', 'climax or end of story card' and build a structure to your plot. Just five cards will give you a main character, there goal, the obstacle they have to overcome, how they deal with the obstacle and the end result.

For the following story I used a ten-card structure. For the theme of the story; a major card, for the main character and his helper I chose two cards, one court and one major card. For his goal I chose one minor card. For what he was expecting from life I chose another major card and another for the unexpected. For the obstacles he faced and their solutions I used two minor cards. From one minor card came the climax of the story and a last minor card for the final result. Here is a list of the cards I chose to write The Circle.

Theme: **Wheel of Fortune**

Main character: Knight of earth
Helper: **High Priestess**
Goal: **9 of earth**
Expected: **Emperor**
Unexpected: **Hierophant**
Obstacles: **8 of air**
Solutions: **10 of fire**
Climax **Knight of water**
Final result **10 of earth**

THE CIRCLE

Joe moved into Hill Farm in the winter following his 21st birthday. Everything had gone to plan so far - he had graduated from agricultural college in the summer at the top of his class after working as hard as he could for several years. He had taken his qualifications to the biggest landowner in the county - Lord Wilding - and applied for the vacant tenancy of Hill Farm. Of course, he hadn't actually got to see Lord Wilding, but he had got the tenancy, which meant he could go ahead with the next stage of his plan: to ask Marianne to be his wife. But first he had to get the farm sorted out and in order before spring planting and get the house fit for Marianne to live in. The fields were to be planted with wheat and barley and if Joe's first crop next summer were successful enough they could have the wedding after the harvest.

So Joe worked hard through the winter - painting the house and putting up shelves in the places Marianne wanted them. He worked hard on the farm too and when the time came for spring planting he was out from early morning till darkness fell. It wasn't until May, as the evenings grew warm and pleasant, that Marianne could persuade him to let up and relax a little.

"Everything you planted is up and growing Joe, you can't do anything else for it, so let's go down the pub and have a few drinks. Our friends have forgotten what we look like."

Realising that she was right Joe agreed. They walked through the fields and over the hill to the village pub. Joe couldn't help checking as he went that each field was growing well. When he was satisfied that all was as it should be he led Marianne into the smoky bar.

They had quite few drinks in the end. A couple they knew from college were in there and they sat laughing about old times and the drinks kept flowing. Jo felt ill on the way home - he told Marianne he could see flashing lights over one of his precious fields. Marianne said that that was what ten pints of beer did to you after several months of sobriety.

The following morning Joe woke up with a thick head and little memory of the night before. He set off on his usual routine about the farm. By mid-morning he had reached the edge of the field at the top of the hill that gave the farm its name, planning on stopping there for a much needed drink before he checked out the field in the valley. He was raising the bottle to his lips when something in the lower field caught his eye. He dropped the bottle and stared down, amazed at what he saw. He blinked his eyes and rubbed them but when he opened them it was still there. There was a circle in the middle of his field. The crop was laying down in a circle formation. This must have happened last night when he was in the pub - he realised. Everything had been ok when he and Marianne had walked to the village - he remembered looking to check. He swore softly -someone had damaged his crop while he had been drinking, what was he going to say to Lord Wilding? With a sinking heart he walked down the hill to take a closer look. As he grew closer to the circle he realised how big it was - the outer ring was at least ten meters across - it had looked smaller from the hilltop. Joe paused and looked around him - how had they got in - there were no paths of down trodden plants leading to the circle - only where he himself had walked. Puzzled, he walked forwards again - perhaps it was animals - although if it were - they weren't acting like he had learned in college. Steeling him to look at the damage done to the plants he stared into the pressed down area. This was getting weird - the plants weren't broken down - they weren't broken at all - they were just, sort of bent. Joe frowned, there had to be some explanation for this. There had to be a solution too, and Joe needed to find it. Stepping away from the strange circle he headed back towards the farmhouse to consult his college books. He was still poring over them when Marianne arrived late in the afternoon.

"What are you doing Joe? I've been ringing your mobile all day and it isn't even switched on". Joe looked up from the book he was leafing through, dispiritedly.

"What's wrong?" said Marianne.

"I found something in the field over the hill and I'm trying to find out what it is," he said "Without much success". "What was it you found?" "I'm not exactly sure…….. it's like a circle……….." He looked at her, helplessly, not sure quite what else to say about it.

"A crop circle?" she said, eyes lighting up with interest. He stared at her, dumbfounded.

"What the hell is a crop circle?" "Well, I'm not sure exactly……… they're some kind of mysterious phenomena". Angry now, Joe threw down the book. "Come on now Marianne - you know all that mystic nonsense cuts no ice with me. This isn't a joke you know - I'm only on trial and Lord Wilding could throw me out if I can't look after the farm properly."

"Joe, it isn't mystic nonsense. I read about it in the Daily Mail a while back. Some politician - I can't remember which one, but a respectable one, had one appear on his land and the papers took photos and there was a serious research thing going on. There's bound to be something about it on the Internet, anyway."

Joe still wasn't happy. "Probably a load of cranks with silly web pages" he said "Anyway, it might not be one of those."

"Well, take me to see it then - I do remember the photo in the paper." Joe didn't speak as they made their way to the top of the hill. Marianne kept quiet too until he pointed downwards at the perfect circle, with the crop laying down as if it had been gently brushed in a beautiful spiral pattern.

"Joe, it looks just like the one in the paper" she said quietly, awed by what she saw. Joe took a deep breath. "Let's go turn on the computer then."

Within a couple of hours an e mail was on its way to report the appearance of the circle to one Harry Bridges - an apparent expert on these matters. Joe was somewhat mollified by the amount of input from scientists and respectable researchers on the Internet, although still uneasy about the presence of the circle.

Marianne looked up from one of the pages she had printed off. "They take the measurement of the patterns that have been appearing and samples of the plants to be tested biologically" she said. "Any results published? "said Joe. Before she could reply the computer bleeped. "We've got an answer already!" she said. "That was quick," said Joe, clicking on the 'read' icon. "He'll be here tomorrow morning".

A dusty red van drove into the farm the following morning and a short stocky man got out. Friendly brown eyes that crinkled in a weather-beaten face greeted Joe and Marianne, their owner thrusting out a warm square hand to shake theirs. "Good morning, good morning, Harry Bridges... I've come about your circle".

"So what exactly do you mean by earth energies?" asked Joe after lunch that day. "The earth isn't just a dead lump of stuff you know son" said Harry. "If it were nothing would grow here, you know that. Lines of energy cover the whole world and where these lines meet and cross the energy is stronger in the earth.

What I mean is that we have noticed that the earth energies in the circles and patterns that have appeared so far is different to that not in the circles. The plants are changed by this energy too - not damaged as you saw - but slightly different in their make-up".

"So what does that tell us?" asked Joe, still unable to grasp what Harry was talking about. "It tells us that whatever is making these patterns appear seems to be causing the changes and we don't know for sure just what it is, it might be the energy lines, some think it is extra-terrestrials trying to contact us, it might even be the Earth herself communicating with us - whichever you choose to believe."

"Why do you think it's appeared here Harry?" asked Marianne, intrigued by the old man's knowledge. "It's probably a place where the ancient peoples had a stone circle or sacred place. They were much more in tune with the land than people nowadays - they knew how to feel its energy. So much of that knowledge is forgotten but people are beginning to think that these circles are a way of drawing our attention to the need to rediscover what the ancient people knew - the secrets of the land".

"So what do I do about it?" said Joe, running his hands through his hair. "Well it'd be a great help if you'd let the croppies - the measurers and so forth, come and investigate it, but other than that nothing, son, well, nothing till harvest time then you mow it down with all the rest of the field".

"Oh Joe- we'll have to let them find out more- this is so exciting!" "I'd have to get Lord Wilding's permission," said Joe, still dubious. "Of course you would, son," said Harry. Most landowners do give permission, and it isn't in the researcher's interest to cause damage. But you think about it, sleep on it and let me know what you think tomorrow."

The dusty red van drove off into the distance.

Joe did think about it. His first instinct was to just keep quiet and mow the thing down at harvest time but Marianne was gradually persuading him to at least speak to Lord Wilding's office about it. Reluctantly he left a message on the answer phone that he hoped wouldn't make Lord Wilding think he was a complete lunatic and went, exhausted, to bed. He didn't sleep well that night, he was unable to get the damn circle out of his mind and it was in the early hours before he fell into a restless doze. The phone ringing brought him woozily from the bedroom just before eight. A snooty voice informed him that it was usual procedure to allow Mr Bridges and his team to carry out their research when these events occurred. Amazed, Joe stared at the phone, too surprised to answer, but the voice disconnected promptly relieving him of the need to.

"Well if they said 'usual procedure', then it must have happened there before, Joe" said Marianne, when a stunned Joe phoned her. "But why didn't someone tell me?"

"I don't know love, but we had better follow procedure and inform Harry hadn't we?"

By the time Harry Bridges dusty red van was seen heading towards Hill Farm three days later, Joe was haggard from lack of sleep and three more circles had appeared in the field.

"It is possible that you've made the smaller ones appear yourself Joe, with all that worrying about it. What affects plants also affect people and you saw the plants with your own eyes didn't you? According to the evidence a kind of interaction between the circles and people does seem to be going on. Something like this did happen the year before last a few miles away? One of the groups held a meditation there and a pattern came in the next field". "Don't tell Marianne that, Harry, or she'll drive me mad".

"There isn't nothing new age about that son, people were tuning into the land and focusing on its energy thousands of years before the hippies thought of it. Why don't you come down and help us measure it - see how it feels to walk around the circles?" Unable to find the energy to make an excuse Joe followed Harry down the hill. Marianne was already at the bottom.

"Shall we walk round them Joe?" She held out her hand, without speaking Joe took it and followed her into the circle. A hush seemed to descend around them as they stood there, then Harry's voice spoke:

"From the soles of your feet Joe, feel it."

"Warm..." said Joe, still holding Marianne's hand. She stood, still and silent beside him.

"Good," said Harry "Now feel it rising..."

"Yes... up... swirling... turning..." he faltered.

"Spiral" said Marianne, softly.

"Yes" said Joe-opening his eyes and looking at Marianne.

"Got it!" said Harry, although neither of them heard him.

This is only the story of the beginning for Joe and Marianne, the beginning of a lifelong quest for the lost knowledge of the land that touched them that day in the circle. By the time Joe was 40 he knew almost as much as Harry Bridges. Harry had spent the last years before his retirement grooming Joe to take his place. And Marianne? Marianne took their children and eventually, their grandchildren to see the circles and swirls that appeared. She told them the stories of their ancestors and how Mother Earth was showing them her magic now.

Joe never did mow them down at harvest time- he went around them rather than desecrate their beauty.

The symbol of the circle in the Wheel of Fortune gave me the theme for my story and as Joe was an earth knight my circle manifested in the earth as a crop circle, something Joe could see and touch. The Emperor filled the role of Lord Wilding, the distant landowner and the wise Hierophant became Harry Bridges who taught Joe what he needed to know, helped by Joe's intuitive wife Marianne, inspired by the High Priestess. Joe's goal was the confidence in life and the security of the nine of earth but the tricky eight of air trapped him in a blind and ignorant state. Casting off his disbelief and imagined constraints as depicted in the ten of fire solved the problem for him, enabling him to transform into the visionary knight of water. This brought him full circle to another ten, this time that of earth, a card that emphasizes the magic that lies in our earthly reality, that so many of us miss. Joe expected the security of the nine of earth but the Wheel of Fortune progressed him to the ten - Joe certainly ended up with much more than he had expected as he allowed the Wheel's vibrant energy to course through him

UNSTRUCTURED METHOD

You do not need to use a formal plot structure to use Tarot for storytelling. You can, if you prefer, just select a group of cards and work with them in a more intuitive way - opening to their energies and allowing them to tell you the story. You will find that just sitting looking at the cards and maybe moving them around a story will begin to emerge. The symbols and the images will point out the way the story unfolds. I used this method to write the following story.

BIRDS

Cards selected:

5 of fire, Cunning Man, Wise Woman, 7 of water, Soul Mates, 2 of air, 9 of air.

Mack stared into the fire, the wind down the chimney made the blaze flare up. He poked the heart of the fire with an old iron poker.

"Go on burn" he told it; Mack was master of his own fire, if no longer master of much else. He could order its burning - he would dammit!

His focus turned back towards the source of his distress - he had heard news today, news that had disturbed him. She was back. Grace. The love of his youth, his only real love. His lost love. Back after so many, many years. Back now it was too late. That was what had upset him, made him angry. The rumour he had heard was that she had come home to die. But that was typical of her; rumour and mystery were what she was all about, what she had always been about.

He laughed wryly; she was probably sitting up there in her abandoned ancestral home laughing her socks off at him and everyone else who had always been fascinated with her doings. He shook his head; she must be as old, gray and wrinkled as he was. She could be dying. That thought made him feel sad, he had lost her all, those years ago. He had driven her away with his pig-headed ways and his determination to direct and control the magic they had made together and never again had he been able to make magic like that with anyone.

Restlessness filled him and he dragged his arthritic bones up from his chair and slowly walked over to the window. He looked out across the darkness. At one time, he could see her house from here, but not now, an industrial estate now stood in the way. Once you could hear the birds that nested by the lake on her property calling, as she had called him. He stared at the dark sky above instead and wondered what she was doing, and what he should do. The germ of an idea sprouted in his mind - should he go there and see her?

She sat in the kitchen of her family's old house drinking a cup of herbal tea. Memories crossed the screen of her mind as she sat there. Some happy; children running through the house playing together, Grandma Beaton telling stories by the fire. They used to say Grandma Beaton was a witch. Grace smiled; people had said that about her too, still did as like as not. Mack came to mind - he had always called her a witch. Dark eyed dynamic Mack; she wondered how he was now. She had used to worry that he would become totally corrupt with his power, destructively corrupt. But he was probably just some crusty old git like most men of their age.

She wondered if he still lived in the old place. She couldn't see him letting go of it that had never been Mack's way of things. She felt a pang of regret. He had let go of her. But then she hadn't given him a choice; she had just retreated from him when he refused to accept her truth. She sighed, she should have stood her ground and acted really, running away had not been the answer; the other worlds she had visited had always lacked one thing - Mack or anyone like him. Although so different in many ways they were birds of a feather and they had belonged together for life, like the swans by the lake, and both of them had wasted it- following their differences rather than what had united them. Flying away on different winds. If only they could have reached a compromise they could have brought their joint visions to reality. Why had it taken her till now to really see the truth? She, who was supposed to be wise. She remembered how good they had been together in the beginning, how in tune with each other they were, she only had to open her mind and listen, maybe call him, and he would be there listening, speaking to her as no one else ever could. She wondered if she could still do that. She sat back in the old rocking chair where Grandma Beaton used to sit and took another sip of her herbal tea.

"Mack" she said "Are you there?"

He stumbled out of the doorway into the dark night - he was going, walking stick and all, she needed him, wanted him, he had heard her call across the distance of years at last. He struggled against the wind up the path focusing all his determination on getting to her.

She sat in her chair, her intuition open, hearing him come. Her heart gave a little leap in her frail old chest. At last, at last!

At dawn the following morning any one out of bed might have seen two birds fly into the air, circle round each other as if in greeting and fly off together. Anyone awake in other ways might have seen the two spirits that accompanied the birds as they soared above the sleeping body of the earth, together at last.

MAJOR ARCANA STORIES

THE TRAVELER
Inspired by The Fool

The Doors of Time opened and I stepped through to a place of marvelous beauty. As the Doors closed behind me and retreated into the Mists I gazed around me in wonder. Green hills with scattered clumps of white and orange flowers rose around my dog and me, and a yellow sun shone brightly in an azure sky. I put my bag down and leaned on my stick breathing in the fresh clear air and enjoying the symphony of birdsong. The dog scampered around barking joyfully, first in one direction, then another and then running back to me as if to say "Which way shall we go?". Now there was a question that needed an answer. There was something about that that I was supposed to remember. As I stood there wracking my brains, the dog scampered over and picked up my bag in her mouth, dropping it at my feet. As I looked down at the bag I saw a large purple question mark had been sewn onto the indigo fabric. Thanking the dog for her help I sat down on the grass and took the bag from her mouth. I opened it and reached inside. My hand touched something and I drew out a small, red, heart shaped box. Carefully I lifted the lid and a tune began to play. Sweet notes drifted around us in an enchanting melody and the dog and I began to move to its rhythm. Then suddenly it stopped. The dog sat down and looked at me expectantly.

"What?" I said, not knowing what I was supposed to do next. Of course, she didn't answer, just looked at me with her wise eyes.

I looked back at the little box. The lid wasn't fully open. Looking closer I could see there was something obstructing it. It was a piece of paper, folded into a tiny square. Carefully I unfolded it. There was something written on it. Holding it up to the light I deciphered the words

"Dear Traveler," I read," that must be me" I said to the dog, who woofed in reply. "By the time you read this message you will have forgotten where you came from and who you are. This was the price you paid for your passage". So that was what I was supposed to remember! I was to have no memory.

And it was right, I tried for a few minutes to recall where I had come from and I couldn't- not a thing, just blank space. I tried to remember my name and again - nothing, I couldn't even remember the dog's name.

"Oh well, we'll just have to be Traveler and Dog" I said to her and turned back to the message.

"You may also have forgotten the purpose of your journey" I read. I stopped to consider, and yes, I had forgotten the purpose of my journey. That was a damn fool thing to do! Whatever had made me do such a thing? I couldn't remember that either. Perhaps this message would remind me. I picked up the paper again: "As is usual for these journeys, a musical clue has been provided for you.

Follow the tune and you will find what you seek." And that was it, the end of the message. No map, no name of a person to guide me, not even a signature to say who wrote the message, just the tune. This was crazy, but what else could I do? I opened the lid of the box again and a stream of notes flowed out like a ribbon of rainbow coloured beauty. The dog and I leapt eagerly to our feet. We were off ... following the tune...crazy or not...

WOLFMAN
Inspired by the Cunning Man/Magician

I wandered far on that first day of my exploration of this new land I had arrived in; across green fields and up and down hills and valleys. For a long time I saw no other creature until I approached a small copse of pine trees, where a drift of smoke led me to suspect that there was someone around. Eager for company, the dog and I headed towards the trees. It was quiet under the trees and I looked around me, puzzled now I could not see the drifting smoke to guide me. The dog sat down as if waiting for me to tell her what to do, but

I was at a loss. Then something made me turn and before me in the clearing I saw a wolf. Huge and shaggy, he stood between two trees looking at me. Then, as I stood paralysed with fear, his form began to waver in the still air and before my incredulous eyes; he sort of slipped, from being a wolf to being a man. He was tall and sparely built with long grey hair and piercing eyes. He wore a dark red cloak with a collar of soft fur, like wolf skin.

"Welcome Traveler, to this land" he said. I did not answer him immediately, so stunned was I at what I had seen. His steady gaze continued to rest on me as I struggled to gather my scattered wits. At last some coherence returned;

"Is everyone here like you?" I burst out "Can they all change shape?"

He smiled.

"They are like they are, and I am like I am. We are all unique. And anyone can change their shape if they will. Even you."

"Really?" I said "But I would have no idea how to do such magic"

"Do you know of magic?" he enquired, sitting down on a fallen tree trunk and gesturing to me to join him.

"No, I don't know of it, I just know that magic is." I answered, not sure how I even knew that.

"A good starting point" he said "There are many different kinds of magic, shape changing is only one of them. But all magic is about changing something, shifting the energy around, like when you saw me shift from wolf to man, or when you arrived here from a different place."

"Do you think that could be why I came here, to find out about magic?" I asked him.

"Only you can find out why you came here" he said.

Slightly disappointed in his response, I asked him to tell me more about magic and how he had become so skilled at it.

"To find the magic in this world you have to find it within yourself first." he said "Your body, your feelings, your thoughts and desires are all magical tools that you can learn to use. Becoming aware of and able to use well, the magic within yourself, is the first step, the first change. The second is to recognize this same magic in the world around you and align with it for the good of all life forms"

"How many steps are there?" I asked, fascinated by the aura of wisdom and power around him.

" Do not be too eager, Traveler" he said " Knowledge by itself is not enough, skill comes only with dedication and practice and it would be foolish and dangerous to dabble in what you do not yet understand. Take time to explore yourself and your world if you want to discover magic"

"How long would it take me to be as skilled you are?"

He laughed at me.

"What, many years?" I said, guessing by his laughter that I had asked a silly question.

"Many lifetimes, Traveler, and still no end of the road in sight."

"Can you at least point me in the right direction on that road?"

"I already did "was his answer.

When I turned to look at him he had disappeared as if by magic, and I began to wonder if I had imagined the whole encounter. Then I spotted a scrap of dark red fabric from his cloak, snared on a fragrant pine needle. Carefully, smiling to myself, I put these in my bag so I could take a reminder of his magic with me. I took a deep breath and decided to continue my journey; I had much to think about along the way now. He had made me feel excited about it. This world was full of possibility, so I got up from the tree trunk and set off on the road at a brisk pace, with the dog trotting happily by my side, to see what, or who, else I could find in this strange land.

THE PAINTED WAGON
Inspired by the Wise Woman/High Priestess

The day was drawing to a close as I walked along the road. The sky was turning from azure to indigo. The dog suddenly stopped and sniffed the air and as my gaze lowered from the sky I noticed ahead of me, to one side of the path, a painted wagon. Curiosity led me forward without hesitation to investigate, with the dog trotting along by my side. As I drew closer I heard a woman singing. Although I was not near enough to hear the words I knew she was singing of something magical and her song drew me closer like a magnet, releasing its hold only when I stood spellbound before her. She sat at the top of the tiny steps that led up to the doorway to her wagon, a silver beaded curtain shimmered behind her, veiling the inside from my view. Her long black hair, half covered by a silk scarf, shone with the reflection of the silver beads. She wore large hooped earrings that glittered against her dusky skin, and her eyes were of a brilliant aquamarine and I knew if I could dive into them I would become all knowing. All this I knew without a word having passed between us. Calmly and silently she regarded me, shuffling the pack of strange cards she held in her slender hands, the jeweled rings on her fingers flashing.

"I have been waiting for you, Traveler" she said. I stared back at her. It was hard to know if she was old or young, she had an air of timelessness about her and somehow I felt that she knew me.

"Who are you?" I asked, feeling that somehow, I should know the answer.

"I am Gypsy" she said, cutting the cards and placing them in two piles on the small shelf beside her. A thrill of excitement ran through me, I knew that gypsies were people who travelled. Perhaps she could tell me which road to take.

"That is not the purpose of our meeting, your path is not the same as mine" she said, as if she had read my mind." I travel inner roads. My journeys take me to other realms, places where signposts are unclear and direction is decided by instinct and intuition."

Disappointed, I lowered my gaze from her face and as I did I noticed for the first time the wheels on her wagon. The rims of the wheels were gleaming silver, like the beads, and engraved with tiny pictures and symbols. What she said must be true for these delicate wheels would not be so if she travelled the roads my dog and I had walked in this land. Puzzled, I returned my gaze to hers; "Then what is the purpose of our meeting?" I asked. She smiled at me gently.

" Learning to ask the right questions will be a great help to you on your journey, " she began" The purpose of our meeting is for you to learn that, though my path is not the same as yours, my way of travelling has many similarities and I travel for some of the same reasons as you do. I walk the inner roads seeking knowledge and understanding. I seek to open doors that have remained closed to me before."

What she said felt very right- I was journeying through this land seeking knowledge, I did want to understand why I was here, and it was like opening closed doors in a way. The aquamarine eyes twinkled at me;" Would you like to ask another question?" she said

Straight away I said I would, and then paused to think. What should I ask?

"What can I learn from you that will help me on my journey?" I said, at last.

"How to find the guidance you need from within yourself," was her answer. She clearly saw my puzzlement and smiled again.

"Choose a card from each of these piles and I will show you what I mean."

The first card I drew showed a night sky, shadowy forms and fleeting images moved across a sea of stars, making shapes and patterns among the planets, I thought I heard the song she had called me with, but broke the spell when I looked up from the card. She indicated the second pile to me and I chose my second card. This card showed a bright morning and a fresh green land, so real I felt I could touch it. I was sure it was the land I travelled now.

"What do you see?" she asked me.

"I see two different worlds; one dark, mysterious and unknown, one light, clear and very real to me"

"Combine the gifts the worlds of night and day offer you and you will learn all you need to know for your journey, Traveler" she said. "Now rest til morning comes when you shall continue your journey".

I dreamt that night, with the dog curled at my side, of the painted wagon travelling a starlit road, and I knew before I woke that she was gone. But like all gypsies do, she had left me a lucky charm. In my hand I held a tiny wagon just like hers, but made from a curious metal, that at first I thought was silver but when the morning sun shone on it, was gold.

WILD ROSE
Inspired by the Mother Nature/Empress

They had told me in the village that I could buy milk and bread and maybe some fresh eggs in the farm further up the lane. The thought of breakfast spurred me on and whistling the dog to me I headed off into the fine spring morning. It had rained the night before and the hedgerows glistened with raindrops sparkling like diamonds in the sunshine. The lane was long and winding but I enjoyed the walk, spring flowers decorated the edges of the fields with cheery colour and birds sang a merry song from the treetops. At last I came to the track that I had been told led to the farm and slipping a lead on the dog I turned onto it. The farm yard was deserted apart from a few hens scratching about so I approached the farmhouse and knocked on the solid wooden door. Then I heard bells ringing behind me and a voice said "Hello there, traveler" in a soft country burr. I turned round to see a woman standing by a large white cow with bells around her neck.

"Sorry I wasn't in, I had to go and find Daisy, she wandered off again." I stood, tongue tied, stunned by this woman's beauty. She had golden skin and wide clear eyes. Her dusty pink dress clung to a body full of promise and a red ribbon held back a mass of shining hair.

"Was it milk you were wanting?" she asked.

"Err ... yes please "I stuttered

"Come into the barn then and Daisy will give you some, nice and fresh."

The dog, who I had forgotten all about, pulled on her lead. She clearly wanted to follow the woman, who didn't seem anything like a farmer's wife.

"Have you come from the village?" she asked as she perched gracefully on the milking stool. I was so mesmerised by her supple hands milking the cow that I didn't hear what she had said.

"Pardon... erm... sorry I didn't..." I blushed like a fool. When had I become so clumsy and awkward?

Why was I paralysed by this woman's presence?

"Oh you can speak then, I thought the cat had got your tongue. I asked if you had come from the village" she repeated.

Stung by her mockery, I felt my skin turn hot again and tears filled my throat. Would she be cruel to me?

"Oh don't mind me, I 'm only teasing. "she said. She smiled, and like the sun coming out on a rainy day, I felt better." You must be tired, why don't you sit a while?"

Gratefully I sank onto the stool she offered me. She was right, I was tired. So was the dog, who had settled herself at the woman's feet, and we were hungry. As if she read my mind the woman spoke again.

"I'll get you some breakfast when I've milked Daisy, and I'll feed the dog."

There seemed no need to answer so I didn't and she carried on with her task. The morning grew warmer and the rich smell of hawthorn drifted into the barn. The woman began to hum as she worked and then to sing. I had never heard such a song; it was as wild and beautiful as she. It was song of earth, wind, rain and fire, of sun moon and stars. It was a journey of soaring love and searing pain, of birth and death that mingled effortlessly and seamlessly with a strong and joyful heartbeat.

I felt myself becoming one with the song and the singer and my spirit lifted as the melody ran across fragrant green fields like velvet under my bare feet, through a shining sea that soaked me with its silver spray, to fly me on the highest wind over an icy mountain kingdom to a fiery red sunset. I came to myself as the sunset faded, realising that the woman's voice had fallen silent. She and the white cow had gone. I felt bereft, cold and empty without the woman and her song to fill me. How could she leave us after what she promised? Who was this woman anyway and why did I feel like this about her? I did not understand any of this. My belly rumbled and the dog whined in her sleep. Rubbing my bleary eyes I noticed on the stool where the woman had sat there was a basket. Eagerly I reached out to it. A crusty loaf, still warm from the oven, brown speckled eggs and rich frothy milk, red shiny apples and a meaty bone for the dog. She had not forgotten us, she did care!

Without moving from where we sat the dog and I ate our fill. Never before or since have I tasted such food, it fed both my body and soul; and well before the basket was empty I was satisfied, refreshed and renewed. As I put the remainder of the loaf aside to eat later I noticed something else in the basket. It was a wild rose. I pricked my thumb on its tiny thorn and sucked the spot of bright red blood that was the colour of her hair ribbon. Joy filled my heart as I understood at last who she was. And I knew she that loved me, for she had left me her emblem. The farmyard was still deserted when the dog and I left the barn, but it did not matter, I knew she was there somewhere and always would be, come rain or shine. I heard the white cow's bell as the dog and I walked back down the track, Wild Rose in my button hole.

THE CASTLE
Inspired by the Lord of the Wild/Emperor

"Hey, you!"

I heard a voice shout as I climbed to the top of a green hill. I looked up, seeking the owner of the voice, to see a tall figure above me. I could not see him clearly at first; my eyes were dazzled by the sun that shone behind him. As I drew closer I saw he was a tall strong looking young man with bright golden hair.

"Can you go and stand at the other side of the summit with this" he said, handing me a piece of string, "I need to measure this side of the building."

"What building?" I said, taking the string and walking across the plateau at the top of the hill.

"The castle I am building" he answered, as if it should have been obvious to me.

I suppose my puzzlement was clear on my face, for there was no building where we stood, or any signs of one being built.

" Sit down, " he said and for some unknown reason I obeyed him as I had with the measuring string, wondering to myself as I did so; what was it about him that I naturally followed his orders?

"Let me explain;" he began, sitting down beside me, crossing his long powerful legs. "One day I shall wear a crown. The wearing of this crown is a sacred trust, it brings power but it also brings responsibilities. One of those responsibilities is to provide a rallying point for the people of the land. So I shall build a castle for them. This is a good place, high on this hill, where they can see it clearly for miles around." An eagle flew above as he spoke and he raised his hand in greeting, pausing to watch the bird wheel across the sky.

He pointed to the valley on the other side of the hill. "See the river flows by, so we will have water. He gestured to the large flat area at the summit of this hill; "A natural place for a fire to warm a large hearth" he said" And in the north there shall be a stout oak door"

"What will you build your walls from?" I asked for I could see no building materials

He smiled at me, enthusiasm firing his eyes, and pointed to a line of young trees of many different species all growing close together on one side of the hill just beneath the line of the summit.

"The Army of the Trees has sent its warriors to protect this side" I stared at them, amazed, for what he said made sense, they did look like a group of warriors assembled to stand guard.

"I have working parties for the other walls- the Bards are coming from the west to sing a wall of crystal light for one, another party journey to a holy isle to bring a sheet of shining glass, and giants carry huge stones from the quarries of the gods"

He built the castle in my mind's eye with his words .I too, quickened with enthusiasm for this marvellous place. And I marveled that one who seemed to be so young could command such forces, Bards and giants indeed!

"My people will assemble then and we will live in peace and plenty. You can stay here with us if you want to. "He said "You can join our clan if you are willing to work for your keep. You will find my ruling just and fair, for society can be no other way and the crown compels it's wearer to be this way, or pay the price"

His offer tempted me- how good it would be to be a part of this, so much I could learn and discover in a safe and secure company. How did the Bards sing a wall of crystal light I wondered? What kind of giants were this young man's coworkers? It all sounded so exciting.

But something told me no- the time was not right for me to settle in one place, I knew I had to travel on.

Regretfully I turned him down but took the friendly hand he offered in farewell. As I grasped his hand I mine and looked into his eyes I saw him as he would be in years to come- a jeweled crown upon his head, his features more firmly set by Time's hand, and threads of silver through his golden hair.

"Should you return, we will be here" he said, inclining his noble head at me, and I knew they would.

THE POET
Inspired by the Interpreter/Hierophant

I heard a voice, chanting words in a language I could not understand, carried to me on the wind as I toiled up a steep hill. Wondering who the voice belonged to; I pushed my legs harder to reach the crest of the rise. As I climbed I could see a stone gateway ahead. This was where the voice seemed to be coming from. I could see smoke rising from between the pillars that formed the gateway. As I stepped towards it I saw the source of the voice, a tall figure, through a haze of smoke.

"Greetings you who travel here step forward now and have no fear" said a deep male voice.

A little puzzled at his strange mode of speech and the fact that I could now understand the words he said, but reassured by his friendly tone, I stepped forward. The smoke drifted upwards as he spoke and I could see him more clearly. He was a strange looking one; tall and dark, clothed in robes of red and green and crowned with a wreath of oak leaves. The arms he held out in welcome were covered in tattoos of a whirling design that seemed to move across his skin of their own volition.

"Who are you?" I asked, feeling just a little daunted now.

"I am the Poet who remembers the rhymes

The one to guide you through this place and time"

"You can guide me?" I asked; guidance was something I could do with.

"If you would travel through night and through day I am the one who remembers the way", was his answer, which I took to be a yes. Trying to adapt myself to his curious way of communicating, I thought carefully about my next question. I knew I had to make the most of my strange advisor, I felt an excitement deep inside me that told me he spoke the truth.

"How will you guide me "I said after a lengthy pause. His light coloured eyes sparkled and he answered me with a smile; "With wisdom from the ancients that relates to today I will point out the connections that mark out your way".

It occurred to me that there were connections that had marked my journey so far. I felt a growing sense of kinship with him as he seemed to touch chords within me with his words.

"How can I recognise these connections as I travel on?" I said.

"By looking and listening, by feeling the air by seeing the patterns in sun, moon and star respecting tradition, though it must not hold you back you must move on to seek what you lack by taking directions north, south, east or west by learning to realise your heart knows best by living your story in faith, hope and trust accepting the challenge to do what you must".

He beckoned me forward;" Accept my blessing; to wish you farewell my gift to you is this rhyming spell".

He touched my lips with his cool fingers and I felt tingling as a great surge of energy flooded my being, as if his words sang through my veins. Then he was gone and the stone gateway was no more. But I was left with the memory of his unforgettable rhymes chiming through me as I turned to continue my journey.

DUET
Inspired by the Soul Mates/Lovers

There was a long queue of people blocking the main street through the small town I had wandered into that morning. I asked a woman what they were all waiting for.

"For the ticket office at the theatre to open" she answered," There's a performance tonight no one wants to miss"

More people shoved from behind and I became a part of the queue as there was no way I could move out of it.

"Who is performing?" I asked the woman, curious as to who could have so many people wanting to watch them sing or dance or act in a play.

"It's Duet" she answered, looking at me as if I was crazy for not knowing. There was a shout from the rather distant front of the queue that seemed to mean the ticket office had opened, and we all moved forward with a lurch. Well, I thought to myself, if Duet is that good I had just as well get a ticket too, seeing as I'm here. I should enjoy a good performance.

A couple of hours later, after much jostling and pushing I walked away from the ticket office of the small theatre with my ticket in my hand. During my sojourn in the queue I had learned a little more of the famous Duet. There were apparently two people involved, two singers, a man and a woman, said to be lovers. Neither had had any success as a solo artist, although both had fine voices, but as Duet, singing together, they were major stars, returning now to give a performance in their home town.

At last the conductor stood, the orchestra played the opening bars of music and the dusty red velvet curtains opened. A hush fell over the audience and I leaned forward in my seat, eager to see the performers emerge on to the small stage. Pale pink and mauve lights danced forward as a woman, with long red hair, wearing a silver dress, emerged from the wings, as she stepped forward the lights changed to gold and blue and her partner, a tall man with long black hair dressed entirely in black, stepped from the opposite side of the stage. The woman sang out a sweet note and began a lilting song, in words I could not understand. As she finished the first chorus the man took over singing a variation of the melody she had begun. On the third verse they joined hands and sang together. The audience gasped at the magic of their combined voices. The song built, with spine tingling beauty, to its crescendo and they turned towards each other, the coloured lights caressing them as they stood centre stage, holding the entire audience captive with awe. After riotous applause another song began and then another, I found myself humming as if I knew the tune and swaying with my neighbours to a delightful rhythm. Again and again they took the audience to ecstatic heights; performing encores to standing ovations until at last they left the flower strewn stage.

I could not leave it there; I could not just wander off into the night without knowing more about Duet and their music and the way they made people feel. I pushed my way determinedly through the milling crowd in what I hoped was the direction of the dressing rooms.

Through a set of swing doors at the bottom of the auditorium bearing the words- No Admission I found myself in a corridor. The sounds of the crowd were muted here and I noticed several doors leading off into what I presumed were dressing rooms.

"What are you doing here? said a voice behind me. I turned to find the theatre manager storming towards me.

"I have to see Duet" I said, without even thinking, "I have a message for them".

As I spoke a door opened in front of me and the red haired woman stepped out. "

"It's all right, Ben" she said to the man. She watched him retreat through the swinging doors and then turned to me.

"What did you want?" she asked
My mouth dried out and I was unable to speak.
"Have I got to guess?" she smiled and my tongue released itself.

"No... I just wanted to see you - your music; I've never heard anything like it- when you sing together something happens..." I stumbled to a halt as the black haired man appeared behind her. Both were good looking people but together they had a stunning glamour.

"Want to know our secret, do you?" he laughed "Come in, come in"

It was as clear as it had been on stage that they were lovers. Although they did not touch each other all the time there was an almost tangible link between them. Each seemed to know what the other would say as if they knew not only each other's voices and bodies but each other's hearts and minds as well.

"Let's try and explain" he began, looking at her "We love each other and we both love what we do" he said and sat back smiling.

"Don't tease "she scolded him "You know it's more than that." She turned to me and smiled again

"Our attunement goes back a long long time and is made from love. We are soul mates and the love that binds us together shows in how we respond to each other as we sing in harmony. So the beauty we co-create shines out to our audiences and they are able to share in the joy we have, in our music and in each other"

"Does everyone have a soul mate?" I asked, longing to have a partner to share such an experience with.

"So they say" she said " But sometimes soul mates can take many lives to find each other"

"Why?" I asked, disappointed at this and imagining lonely souls wandering around for eons of time.

"Many people spend their time feeling like half a person and searching for what is missing" the man broke in." But it is not until you have learned to be whole in yourself, to take responsibility for your own choices, and love and accept yourself, that you can truly love another. And do not forget- love is like music- sometimes we need to hear discordance in order to understand harmony"

" And even if you find your soul mate the relationship will still need work- we still rehearse regularly to keep our voices tuned in harmony" said the woman

"How will I know it is my soul mate if I do meet them?" I asked.

"Somehow, you will be in tune with each other" she said.

As I left the theatre a little later, still humming one of their melodies, I thrust my hands deep in my pockets. In the left hand pocket I found the little red heart shaped box I had carried since my journey began, and suddenly I remembered- it played a melody! Smiling,

I lifted the lid and began to sing in tune.

SAILING
Inspired by Hunter/The Chariot

I came to a crossroads and stood there, puzzling. Which road should I take? I considered my options. The path to the left led up into barren looking hills that to the right led across an empty plain. I could not see where the centre path, directly ahead of me, led to, but it seemed to be the best choice, so dithering no more, I stepped onto it.

I found myself on a path by a river looking down at a strange kind of boat. It was like a kind of water chariot; small and neat with a sheltered area at the front for the sailor to stand. It was painted black and white with the sheltered area a gleaming silver. It was tied to its moorings with a silver rope. Curious, I stepped aboard, calling a greeting as I did. No one answered my call and as I turned towards the bank to seek the owner of this vessel, the silver rope slipped from the moorings and the boat began to move.

Panicking, I lurched to the shelter and grabbed the red painted wheel. I stared around me wildly. There was no one on the river bank, so there was little point in shouting for help. I realised that I would have to try and steer this thing. At least I had found the wheel, if only by accident! I braced my legs and gripped onto the wheel, trying to stop the little boat from drifting. But the wheel was stiff and I didn't know where to steer to anyway. The river appeared to be winding through open country. I took a deep breath trying hard to quell the rising tide of panic inside me and strangely I began to feel calmer.

"Relax," a voice inside me seemed to say "Balance your feet and hold the wheel lightly. Go downstream with the flow of the water".

I loosened my grip on the wheel and balanced my feet and the little vessel began to move steadily along. I began to feel much better. I had

got the hang of it now and it was quite enjoyable travelling on the smooth water. This river must lead to somewhere, after all. Then I looked ahead of me through the window of the shelter and saw rocks! For a moment fear gripped me, then the inner voice spoke again;
"You can get past these rocks, just have a little courage and steer carefully. Much can be learned from dealing with obstacles"

I took heart from this and concentrating fiercely, I steered carefully around the rocks and was much relieved to find the water ahead of me clear. But not for long, soon I found myself negotiating the little boat around a huge tangle of weeds and maneuvering past the remnants of a fallen bridge. These were huge challenges for a novice such as me, but the inner voice I listened to guided me and eventually I managed to pass them all.

The voice had spoken truly, I had learned a lot from this experience about how to sail safely through difficult places, which would be helpful to me on other journeys. Although I was now hungry, thirsty and tired, I had gained a sense of achievement as well as much knowledge, from these trials.

At last I saw lock gates ahead of me and as I drew nearer I saw a silver rope, like the one the little boat had been tied with when I boarded. And I knew then that this part of my journey must be done. I steered the boat in and tied her with the silver rope, realising that I was now a slightly different person from the one who had set out on this little voyage. As I stepped onto the river bank I saw a sign with an arrow pointing to an inn. The inn was called "The Traveler's Rest" so I knew, without doubt, I had landed at the right place.

THE GENTLE MAN
Inspired by Natural Force/Strength

I heard the sound of thundering hooves and a wild neighing as I rounded the bend in the road. Fear filled me and I leapt into the bushes at the roadside to hide myself from whatever terrible creature was coming this way. I scuttled deep into the undergrowth, not caring how the thorns tore at me.

Eventually, I ran out of breath and as I stopped to rest I realised the noise had stopped, I could no longer hear the hooves or the blood curdling neighing. I waited, listening until my pounding heart slowed to its normal rate. Still hearing nothing and hoping that it was safe to do so, I began to crawl out, looking for a gap in the undergrowth to peep through, to make sure whatever I had heard had really gone. Sunlight began to filter through the bushes and I crawled towards it.

I could see a wide clearing in front of me. I stopped in my tracks as I saw a gleaming white horse pawing the ground, she was so white she was almost silver; as if she was made of light- for somehow I knew this was a mare, and a wild one. As she pawed the ground her breath blew like clouds of steam around her beautiful head. Her eyes flashed like lightening, dark and wicked as she kicked her back legs out, screaming wildly, and raced around the clearing. I froze in the bushes. She would trample me for sure, but I was as mesmerised by her beauty as by my fear. She stopped and reared up on her back legs, throwing her graceful neck back she let another wild yell. As she reared I saw that a man was standing in the clearing now. He stood, as still as a tree , just a few feet from her deathly hooves, not reacting to her screams, as if he could not hear her challenge. She stopped, as if she too was puzzled by his quietness and lack of fear. When she fell silent I could hear another noise. The man was making a humming sound, a strange sound, not like a real tune, then it turned to a kind of whinny. The mare lifted her head and took a step towards him, as if she understood him. He turned his head slowly, to look at her, still making a soft whickering sound. Her dark eyes flashed as she gave a neigh in reply, but still she walked towards him as if he called her and he stood still, as if waiting for her. She reached him and my view of him was blocked, for a few minutes the two stood entwined, the light that reflected from her seemed to embrace them both in a bright glow so they looked like one shining figure, and I was dazzled.

Then I saw him turn and begin to walk around the clearing, she watched him for a moment and then she followed him, until they walked side by side with her nuzzling his shoulder as if they were two dear friends, not a wild creature and a man. He stopped again and fed her something he drew from his pocket. Suddenly he spoke aloud; "You can come out from the bushes now, I've told her you mean her no harm" he said. In amazement, I scrambled to my feet and came out into the clearing- I didn't think he knew I was there. "I thought she was a wild creature, I hid because I was frightened" I said

"She is wild" he said "and she could smell your fear, which made her feel fear as well"

"It looked as though you tamed her, without whips or reins" I said" I did not tame her, why would I? Did you not see the beauty in her wildness? There was no need for her to suffer the cruelty of bondage that would turn her passion and courage into a powerful destructive force that would burn her out. "he said "I just spoke to her in her own tongue, with respect, and took away her fear without taking any of her power or her freedom"

The mare turned and looked at me and I saw her eyes were deep dark pools of liquid light, as I gazed into them the fear left me, still awed by her beauty I looked at the man to see if I should approach her.

"Gently now," he encouraged me, beckoning with one hand, stroking her shimmering back with the other. She stood quite still but as my hand touched her I felt her power, her passion and courage, fill me with radiance. Time seemed to halt as this radiance flowed through me and over me, leaving me still glowing when it at last receded and I found myself alone in the clearing.

THE STATUE
Inspired by Healter/The Hermit

I was looking for directions, a signpost or a place to buy a map, when I came across the garden. It was enclosed in shiny black railings and the fragrant shrubs that hung over the open gate seemed to call me in to rest a while from my journey through the narrow winding streets of the old city I found myself in. I stepped through the gate and found myself in a green sanctuary of peace and stillness. A wide tree lined path led through the middle of the garden with benches, as shiny and black as the railings, dotted along it between the trees.

I walked under the emerald canopy to sit on one of these benches and gather my thoughts. There was no one else around so I settled myself comfortably and looked around me. All was peaceful and calm; I could hear a few birds chirping and small animals rustling in the undergrowth. Some of the trees were very old and very beautiful, with many different species complimenting each other. I was musing on the talents of whoever cared for this garden when I noticed that to one side of me, where I had thought a tree stood; there was in fact, a statue. This was not a statue made of stone but one of wood- that had roots at the bottom as if it were still a tree. From the tree roots there seemed to grow first the folds of a cloak, then at waist level; a pair of strong arms, folded in front of the body, hands tucked in the sleeves. The figure was much taller than I, but as I looked up I could see the weathered planes of his face beneath the hood he wore. I read the brass plaque attached to the hem of the cloak- the statue- titled The Hermit- had been carved from the still living remains of an ancient tree that had been damaged in a storm. I touched the folds of the cloak in wonder.

"It looks so real, as if he is still alive" I said, aloud. I had not expected to find such a thing of beauty.

"I am still alive," came the soft voiced reply "I wait in these gardens for those such as you". " I would rather keep moving than be waiting " I said " Aye, most people say that," he said " but sometimes it is wiser to wait".

"To wait for directions? That is what I was looking for when I found you" I said. "Not so much for directions, as for illumination" he answered" Doesn't that take a long time?"

"Time, now there's a thing" he mused "You people are always worrying about time, scurrying along the paths in such a hurry you cannot have time to draw breath. You miss so much worrying about time".

I could see his point- if I had hurried through the garden I would have missed him altogether.

"Time is for spending" he continued" For discussing and learning and growing".
I sat forward eagerly, moving on forgotten, now I wanted to stay and listen to him.
"Tell me..." I urged him. And he told me of many things; of time and seasons and magical elements, of cycles of wisdom encoded in stories in sacred texts, of the lore of the trees and plants that grew around him. His knowledge wrapped itself around me as he spoke, the deeper meanings of his words resounded in my mind, enchanting and enlightening me. I listened, spellbound, until the Moon lit his face like a lantern, and listened more until the rising Sun warmed my sleepy eyes, with gentle rays filtered through the green leaves, and the Hermit stood in silence once more.

Hunger bade me move at last from the shiny black bench and I stretched my stiffened limbs and touched the Hermit's cloak in thanks and farewell. I knew there was no further need for words between us.

I got up and walked away, turning back for a last look at him as I reached the gate, and smiling to see a dove had perched upon his shoulder.

THE MAGIC CIRCLE
Inspired by Dance of Life/Wheel of Fortune

Dark clouds filled the sky and the wind began to rise as I walked across the broad, open plain. I shoved my hands in my pockets and bowed my head, wishing and hoping that I might find somewhere to shelter from what seemed to be an approaching storm. Thunder rumbled in the distance and the air crackled with electricity. To be struck by lightening was all I needed; I thought to myself as I stumbled on blindly, having lost all sense of direction. I seemed to have little choice but to let the wind blow me where it would; then suddenly I bumped against a large stone. Startled, I looked up and saw that the stone stood before a huge circle of stones. Relief flooded through me; maybe here I could find some shelter until the worst of the storm had passed. I hurried towards the circle which seemed to be made of pairs of stones, each with a stone resting on top, like massive doorways. As I approached the nearest stones the wind seemed to abate a little and I noticed that the doorway was covered with what looked like a spider's web. Dare I break through it? I asked myself. Another loud thunderclap wiped all doubt from my mind and I ran towards it, as I reached it the web blew aside like a curtain- inviting me in. No longer hesitant and somehow knowing that this was a place of magic, I stepped through and it was as if I had stepped through to another place. No wind blew here and no storm raged, the sun shone brightly and all was calm and peaceful.

Sighing with relief I looked around me and saw that from each stone doorway a path led to the centre of the circle. Each path was filled with different coloured plants and flowers and at the centre grew a beautiful tree that bore both blossom and fruit. Curious as to how and why this should be, I made my way to the centre and gazed up into the tree. Only silence met my unspoken questions, so I sat beneath the tree and leaned my travel worn self up against it. I began to relax in the stillness at the centre then gradually I became aware that the circle was moving around me, slowly spinning so the pattern of plants and flowers changed and the stone doorways danced a dignified and stately dance. The sun set above me and the stars came out whirling in the sky in the same circular dance. A sense of wonder filled me and I knew I was being shown something special and deeply magical. I felt myself being lifted by unseen hands to join in this mystical dance, and as I danced and whirled I saw past, present and future as one glorious multi coloured pattern.

Everything I knew and would learn slotted into its rightful place and I knew a feeling of ecstasy I had never known before as my spirit soared to previously unknown heights. Then slowly, slowly, I spiraled downwards again and found myself outside the circle, sitting by the stone that marked the entrance. The magic circle was partly concealed by a soft mist and as I tried to peer through the mist I found I could no longer see it. But I felt different; stronger and clearer as if I had somehow grown and expanded. I was no longer tired and lost, but eager, energetic and ready to continue my journey.

TRUE COLOURS
Inspired by The Hooded One/Justice

I came to a signpost as I walked. It bore the name of an ancient market town that I had heard mention of on my travels. I had walked a long way that morning, my feet were sore and my boots were beginning to fall to pieces, the dog was hungry as well, so I decided to head towards the market town the signpost pointed to, and see if I could get what we both needed. Hoping that my boots would make it I set off along the road. I began to hear the bustling noises of the town before I had rounded the hill. The dog raced eagerly forward, her sensitive nose catching the whiff of food before mine did. Calling her back to me for safety's sake I turned the

corner. Before us was a busy market place. Calling the dog to heel again, I decided to get her some food first so that she would settle down while I looked for some boots. I bought a steaming hot pie and taking a quick bite myself, handed the rest to her. While she buried her nose in the rich gravy I looked around me. There were stalls selling fruit and vegetables, shiny pots and pans, rich glowing fabrics. A cacophony of vendor's voices filled the air as they hawked their goods. At last my wandering eyes caught sight of a stall with boots and shoes piled up on top of boxes. Leaving the dog to her meal I walked towards it. There were boots of all sorts on the stall and as I reached for a gleaming, nut brown pair that looked to be about my size, I sensed I was being watched. I turned to see a white owl perched on the thin shoulder of a young man wearing a hooded coat.

" I'd say you need a size eleven in those , friend." he said " We do have them in forest green and old gold as well if you'd like to try them"

I reached into my bag for some coins. The young man reached out his hand to stop me. As he did I saw his thin brown face and earnest expression.

"No money yet- you see if they suit you first".

I put my bag down and bent to remove my old boots while he turned to his piles of boxes and gathered several in his arms to place before me.

"These are all your size," he said, "and these are the colours we have; this one is old gold, a fine soft leather, very flexible and supple, an elegant boot. This is the rich brown, a good tough water proof- you could climb mountains in those. And this is the green, flexible but tough and hardy, ideal for wild country, forest or paved roads-"

It was a difficult choice. I looked at my old boots- they had once been a fine soft leather. I looked to the young man for help.

"Which pair do you think would suit me best? I asked him.

"The choice is not mine, but yours" was his reply

I thought about my journey so far and the kind of lands I had travelled through. I did not know what lay ahead of me but as I mused upon the possibilities I felt my eyes drawn back to the green boots.

"I'll have those." I said

"The green ones? Good choice, friend, they should suit you very well"

I tried on the green boots and found them to be a perfect fit; they felt wonderful - like gentle hands soothing my tired feet. Deciding to keep them on, I reached into my bag for my coins. I held them out to the young man.

"Is this enough?" I asked, hoping fervently that it was.

He smiled at me as he pocketed the coins.

"A fair price, Traveler," he said. I picked up my bag and the dog came bounding over to me. Satisfied with my purchase I turned to take my leave of the young man and his owl.

"Well, I must be off," I said "Can you direct me to the road out of town?"

"I am blind, friend, so have not seen this road you speak of" he said I stared at him in amazement.

"But you knew how much money I gave you... my size... without measuring me ....and you knew what colour the boots were.."

"Honest souls are neither measured, nor true colours known just by physical sight" he said. He raised a hand to stroke the owl and turned away from me, the hood he wore fell forward, concealing his face from my view. Knowing that more had passed between us than ordinary goods, I set off, in my green boots, with the dog bounding along by my side, to find the road ahead.

NO SACRIFICE
Inspired by Silence/The Hanged Man

I saw a flash of yellow as I came near to the lake. I strained my eyes to see, there was an ash tree blocking my view, but then I saw it again- the flash of vivid yellow fluttering in the breeze. Curious as to what it could be I moved nearer, and as I did I saw it was a yellow dress, with a pair of slim legs inside of it. As I moved nearer the owner of the legs scrambled to her feet. It was a young woman with dark skin and delicate, elfin features.

"Are you all right?" I asked

She smiled at me.

"Yes, I 'm fine," she said politely" and you?"

I smiled back.

"I'm fine too" I said, beginning to feel a little silly. "What were you doing?"

"Looking into the lake" she said

"The lake... why?" I asked

"Come and see," she beckoned me past the ash tree "Lay on your belly, hook your foot in the tree root and hang over the bank a bit."

Wondering what could possibly be in the lake, I did as she had told me.

I felt the blood rush to my head as I hung, suspended, over the edge.

"Don't worry, you won't fall in, I've got you, trust me." I felt her hand grasp my thigh.

"Trust you? I don't even know who you are!" I gasped, beginning to wonder if I had stumbled on some kind of crazy person.

"They call me Teresa... Teresa Crane, but never mind that for now, look into the lake"

I looked into the blue depths, searched with my eyes among the murky green reeds

"What is it I'm looking for?" I asked her

"Open your inner eyes" she said and let go of my thigh. I slipped further down the bank, closing my eyes as my head went beneath the surface and then I saw.....a shining island resting in the far distance at the bottom of the lake. I saw exotic trees that bore gold and silver fruit, rivers that ran with the elixir of life. I felt myself being pulled towards it with a deep longing. What was this place?

Had I been here before? Why did I so want to go there? As I questioned myself, my mouth must have fallen open and suddenly I was spluttering and Teresa Crane was dragging me up out of the water.

"You saw it didn't you?" she said, helping me to sit against the ash tree and recover myself.

"What was it I saw?" I asked her, also wondering why I saw it with my eyes closed.

"It is my home" she said," My ancestral home"

"What are you doing here then?" I said

"I have a purpose here "she said "See that tall grey house over there?" My eyes followed her pointing finger and I saw a grim, desolate place, like a dark hulk on the landscape. "A sick old man lives there alone with no one to care for him. I am his nurse.

When he has had his medicine and I know he will sleep for a while I come down here"
"Do you get paid for what you do?" I said

"Paid? Oh no!" she said, as if shocked by the thought "I love the old man, he planted this tree here to shelter the sacred land of the lake people. He lost his health and strength preserving this place for us, so the ones who wandered on foreign shores could find their way home, using this tree as a marker. It is no sacrifice to care for him, but an honour."

"Aren't you lonely out here on your own?" It seemed such a shame for a young girl to be shut in that grim house with only a vision in a lake to enjoy.

"Not really, I talk to the old man, when he is fit to speak he tells me of the days of our ancestors and sometimes I am by the lake when wanderers come so I can show them the way home"

"Don't you want to go home sometimes?" I said, feeling more and more sorry for her, I too was far from home.

" I carry the vision of home within me, and sometimes I can share that vision, that is enough" she said " When the time comes that the old man no longer needs me I will return"

"Take me with you" the words burst out of my mouth before I stop them.

"I have to go," she said" the old man will need me"

She strode off towards the grey house without a backward glance

"Teresa! Wait ..." I shouted after her but she walked on without answering and closed the grey door behind her.

Feeling lost and confused, I sat back down under the tree, to try and make sense of all this. Why had she shown me her home and then disappeared? And why did I desperately want to go there? I stared into the lake, but saw only my own face reflected back at me.

Perhaps Teresa had to be there for the vision to come, I wondered. Perhaps I wasn't meant to go there. But then why had I seen it? No answers to my questions, only silence. After a while I got to my feet and walked away from the grey house and the ash tree by the lake.

There was nothing I could do, only what Teresa Crane did, carry the vision of home within, to look at with inner eyes until the time is right.

Maybe one day I would find the way there....

THE TUNNEL
Inspired by Rebirth/Death

My sharp intake of breathe drew the dog to my side- she too had seen the snake on the path ahead of us. I felt her hackles rise in fear.

The snake lifted its head poised to strike and the dog growled, instinctively I grabbed her around the neck and leapt to one side dragging her with me. As I leapt I hit my head against a tree I had not noticed and lay senseless for what must have been some time. I came to with the dog licking my face. I wondered how long I had lain there, the light had changed, I could not see clearly anymore. I still felt a little groggy from the blow to my head so I sat for a while trying to gather myself to move on before it became fully dark. The dog began to whine, so I struggled to my feet and peered through the increasing gloom to find the path I had been on. I stumbled on to what I thought and hoped was the right path; at least it seemed to lead somewhere, even if I could not see where. The dog stayed close by my side as I pushed onwards, I peered to left and right of me but could see only what seemed to be dead tree stumps and the odd rock, thrusting up out of the ground as if the land was exposing its bones. A chill wind blew in my face as the path widened out into a
broad plain, just a few dark skeletal trees silhouetted against the deepening night. A sibilant wind whispered through the bare branches, mocking me as I stood there, lost. I shivered in the cold, colourless emptiness and felt my spirits sinking, draining away from me. I had no idea where I was.... there was nothing out here... I could die here and no one would know... just lie here in this barren place and fade away and I didn't even know how it had happened.

Then something, I know not what, made me look up and I saw that a woman was standing quietly a few feet away from me. I had not seen or heard her approach, but she must have come from somewhere. Hope surged in me and I stepped towards her. She was veiled, so I could not see her face, and wore a black hooded cloak with a strange pattern woven in red around the edges. On her feet were boots that seemed to be made of snakeskin.

"I'm lost," I said, a little nervously. "Could you tell me the way out of here?"

"There is no way out" she said "Only a way through"

Her voice was familiar from somewhere but I could not think where.

"Where is the way through then?" I asked, beginning to feel confused. She beckoned me to follow her and led me across the plain for what seemed many miles through an endless night until at last we came to the foot of a mountain. She pointed to a gap in the rocks;

"There, Traveler is the way through. It is quite narrow in the middle so you must take off your coat and leave your bag behind."

I did not want to leave my bag behind, or take off my coat, but neither did I want to stay in this strange and frightening place, so I gave both to the woman. I whistled to the dog but to my surprise she did not move.

"Leave her," said the woman "She will find her own way". Reluctantly I gave up trying to persuade the dog.

"Where does it lead?" I asked

"Find out for yourself" she said, then quickly pulled aside her veil and kissed me with blood red lips. I glimpsed her pure white face and a charm that hung around her neck that I had seen before… somewhere… she pushed me into the tunnel's open mouth.

It dipped sharply below the surface, forcing me into a crouching run. It was dim in the tunnel but not as dark as I had expected, I could see enough to move forwards. Then, as I had been told, it grew narrower and tighter. As I went deeper, it was only by breathing in that I could squeeze forward, the rock walls tearing skin from me as I passed. But I could not go back; I had no choice but to struggle on. The passage widened as suddenly as it had dipped at the beginning and suddenly I was through! Bruised and half skinned, but through to a land of living trees in a fresh pale pink dawn, where the grass was green and my dog bounded excitedly over to me. I
laughed out loud- delighted to see her then I noticed that my bag and my coat also lay on the ground. I picked them up wondering how they could have got there. When I tried to put my coat on I found that it didn't fit me anymore although my bag was unchanged. I shook my head in puzzlement but could not figure it out, only the face of the veiled woman came to mind, as if it was something to do with her, so I left the coat there and taking only my bag and my dog I set off on my way.

THE FEAST
Inspired by Inner Child/Temperance

My stomach rumbled with hunger as I trudged along the path, the dog trudged beside me, her tongue hanging out with thirst. Suddenly she stopped panting and sniffed the air delicately.

"What is it girl?" I said

She sniffed again then moved off the path and through some bushes. I followed her before she disappeared, not wanting to lose her in this unknown place. She led me out onto a much wider path than the one we had been on and, still sniffing the air, moved off at a quicker pace. I began to sniff the air too- what was that smell? I asked myself as the aroma grew stronger. It smelt like food, but no food I had ever tasted. Briefly, I wondered if it could be my hunger making me imagine it but the dog had smelt it first, so I hurried on after her with the tantalising smell leading us both on. The path led to a wide clearing in the centre of which was a large black cauldron suspended over a fire, nearby stood a large table covered with a white cloth and scattered with rose petals. Several jugs of sparkling liquid had been placed on the table amongst the petals. The dog ran forward as I stood staring, I called her back and three women turned from their tasks to look at me.

"You two look hungry" said the woman nearest to me, who was gathering twigs from around the clearing to feed the fire.

"We are" I said, my mouth beginning to water at the potent smell from the cauldron.

"Come sit at our table, you are welcome at our feast" said a woman who looked like a twin to the first, as she chose ingredients from a herb basket beside the cauldron and added them to the brew the third woman stirred.

"The food is almost ready" said the third woman, placing a pile of wooden bowls and a serving ladle within her reach.

She was a little taller than the others but also looked like them enough for me to see that they were sisters.

Gratefully I sat down at the table and waited to be served. What luck, I thought as I stroked the dog's head and looked around the clearing. I saw something I hadn't noticed during my preoccupation with the smell of food; the trees around the clearing had little rags and rainbow coloured ribbons tied to them. They looked very pretty and festive. I turned to ask one of the sisters the meaning of these decorations when a steaming bowl of broth was placed before me. All thoughts of ribbons and rags went from me as I dipped my spoon in eagerly. The broth was delicious and I had swallowed several spoonful's washed down with a goblet of the sparkling drink, savouring the wonderful tastes, before I noticed that there were now other guests at the table. I was surprised to see, among the different coloured people, an ethereal looking creature dressed entirely in flowers, accompanied by an elf with pointed ears. A unicorn and a centaur drank from bowls side by side. Do unicorns eat the same food as us? I wondered and glanced over to the lovely creature's bowl. The unicorn raised its graceful head and spoke to me.

"The Sisters feed each according to their need"

I looked around the table and saw, that although all were served from one cauldron, each ate a different meal, only the enjoyment of each guest was the same. The centaur raised his goblet to me in celebration I shook his hand and turned again to the Sisters, a question on my lips as to what magic they performed here. They must know the art of alchemy to do such a thing. Or was this otherworldly food and drink?

The three smiled at me enigmatically and their only reply was;" Eat your fill, Traveler".

I ate my and drank my fill among this strange and wonderful company before reluctantly taking our leave. Neither the dog nor I were troubled by hunger or thirst again for many days.

SHADOWS
Inspired by The Fiddler/Devil

To this day I don't know what made me buy the little harp from the dusty old music shop. It wasn't as if I knew much about music because I didn't. I loved music and flattered myself I could carry a tune with my voice, but had no training in playing an instrument. But there was something about it that drew me. It was in itself a thing of beauty- the proprietor of the music shop had explained to me that it was made of willow as my hand reached out to stroke it's graceful curve. It cost me more than I could afford as well.

"Don't worry friend, you'll earn yourself a crust and a bed for the night with this beauty" said the proprietor, as he saw me counting the few coins left to me while he tuned the harp. "They say the busking's good down by the river "he added, he must have mistaken me for a musician. Just for the sake of it, I headed in the direction of the river when I left the shop, to find a place to at least see if I could coax a tune from my purchase. I sat under a tree well back from the river bank where people strolled watching the buskers and street performers and took the harp from its wrappings. As if they had a mind and will of their own my fingers plucked the strings.

First one note, then another the little harp played to me, rich full notes that rang out into the air. So entranced was I, that I stayed there all afternoon playing my harp and it was almost sunset when I looked up from my music making to see someone standing there, in the lengthening shadows, watching me.

"That's a right natural style o' playing you got there, friend, you ought to come down and play with me and the boys"

Pleased with my apparent musical talent and flattered by his words I scrambled to my feet, straining my eyes to see him in the gathering dusk. My dog whined a warning and I hesitated; "Who are you?" I asked

"Who me? I'm just an old fiddle player". He raised his fiddle and played a merry little tune, reassured I picked up my harp to follow him. The dog whined again and laid down where she was.

"Leave the mutt," he said " We don't want no howling' at the moon while we're playing"

Slightly puzzled at what was unusual behaviour for the dog, I shrugged my shoulders and left her there, her front paws resting on my bag.

My new acquaintance led me down to the waterfront where half a dozen musicians tuned their various instruments around a scrappy fire someone had lit to keep out the coming night's cold. The flames flickered, distorting my view of their faces. I began to feel unsure of myself; I could not see clearly anymore where I was or who I was with. I turned to the Fiddler who had brought me here, but saw only eyes glittering in a dark face and now they looked sinister, not friendly.

A hand pulled me down roughly; "Sit" said a whispering voice that sent a shiver up my spine.

One of them began to beat on a drum, softly at first then louder and louder till it drummed in my brain, tormenting me; I tried to get up and run but could not move, could not hide from the terrible drum beat. Then a wailing bagpipe that drew its breath on searing pain and agony, chained me, while a wild voice cackled screaming, mocking laughter as the Fiddler played me down into dark and dangerous territory, where I knew only madness waited, like a dragon in its lair, to consume me. I felt bits of me shrivel and die as they tore at me like hungry wolves, with their discordant sounds, then suddenly silence, for just a heartbeat....
"Now you Traveler..." said the Fiddler "Play..... play for yer life"

Too weakened to think of defying him, I sobbed in despair as my fingers fumbled uselessly at the harp. How had I been so stupid as to get myself into this? I knew I couldn't play the harp, how could I have been so foolish? The drumbeat started up again, threatening me, taunting me, beating off the remaining heartbeats of my life. As awkward as an automaton, my numb fingers continued to pluck the harp strings. But weak mewling cries were the only sound to accompany the drumbeat.

"What poor pathetic sound is this? "said the whispering voice "We'd have better sport making the hound sing to our tune. What do you think Traveler; shall your hound take your place?"

This obscenity at last roused me from the torpor that had begun to creep through me, the resignation that I faced my death. My dog could not be made to suffer for my stupidity, she had done nothing to deserve this, and adding to my shame was the realisation I had not heeded the warning she had tried to give me.

"No" I shouted aloud, not able to bear the thought of my dog suffering, and my fingers were freed from their numbness. At last the harp joined with me to cry my defiance loud and clear into the night air. My off key notes found their true places
and I played for our lives. I played while the fire died down and the shadowy musicians sat in silence. I played until I heard my dog bark at the rising sun and I knew I was free again.

When full daylight finally came only the Fiddler remained, his companions had all slunk off under the cover of the darkness. My harp had reached the end of its tune on a triumphant note, my dog and I had survived and at last I could see my adversary clearly. There were no more shadows; just a sad, scruffy little man with a battered old fiddle and a look of desperation in his eyes.
"No hard feelings, eh Traveler" he said. And strangely enough, there weren't.

SNAKE PATH
Inspired by Lightening Tree/The Tower

I was weak and tired, my bag weighed heavy on my shoulder, and my feet dragged. My journey had become difficult and I had decided to seek some shelter in this lonely place, somewhere to take refuge from the storm that I could see brewing in the sky. Leaden clouds gathered to threaten me with their sullen darkness, shadowing the light of the day. It was hard to see the road ahead and as the atmosphere grew heavier the task grew harder. But I had to fight on- if I didn't find shelter I would have to bear the full force of the storm.

Panic at the thought of this gave me the energy to stumble on until I came to the bottom of a steep, high hill, which had a strange spiral path, coiling around it like a white snake, leading up to an old stone tower on the summit, where I could see a light flickering. That light in that isolated tower was my only chance; I had to get to it. The wind began to rise as I set upon the spiral path, its icy coldness whipping my hair into my eyes and tugging at my clothes. Trembling with fatigue, I fell on all fours clinging to the tufts of grass at the edges of the path as I climbed. The wind rose higher with a keening cry, like a host of demons was screaming at me, as I inched my way towards the tower and the light. This was no ordinary storm, but one of supernatural power - what had I blundered into? And why?

In fear of my life and crawling like an animal I reached the summit - and the tower. The tower that stood in the calm centre of the storm.

I paused for an instant, to fill my eyes with its safe stone walls, and scrambled gratefully to their shelter. As I stumbled through the empty gap, where a door had once been, the light went out and the wind dropped. There was total silence. Silence so deep and dark I dare not even breathe. Terror held me as still as a vice.

Then the sky roared its thunderous rage, black rain hammered down and white forked lightning ripped the tower from around me, tearing it's ancient stone walls from their anchoring's and tossing them like a child's toys, into the maelstrom. A bolt of energy claimed my body and hurtled me into the darkness like a rag doll.

I had no chance, not even the will to fight, as I became one with the storm. I was surrendered to the elements, and if they should they tear me limb from limb and this was my journey's end, then so be it. I was released from myself and all that I had been.

But I did not die. The storm ended, its wild force spent, and I came to myself again, shaken and bewildered, but whole and unharmed. I rose on wobbly legs and turned to survey the smoking ruins, the white spiral path was littered with debris. But it was calm and peaceful now and I could see the way down. Strangely, my bag seemed lighter and despite my experience, I felt as refreshed as if I had slept a whole night. I had the energy to come back down the hill, on feet that no longer ached. The road ahead was clear to me now, so clear that I could not understand how I had not seen it before the storm. I reached the bottom of the hill and began to walk
away, wondering about the storm and the way it had revitalised me. Had it been the storm? I asked myself, after some distance. Or had it been the tower? I turned around and looked back. I saw, not a snake path up a steep high hill, topped by a smoking ruin; but a gentle green slope, with a winding path of spring flowers that led to its crown, where soft sunlight shone on a small stone building, perched sturdily, all walls and doors intact.

STELLA
Inspired by Source/The Star

I came upon the Star Inn as dusk approached. The sign creaked in the wind as I walked up the road; I smiled to see a silver star on a midnight blue background. It wasn't a fancy place, the paint was peeling a little and it had clearly seen better days but the lights in the windows made it look cozy and I needed a meal and a bed for the night. I pushed open the door. There were a few old men sitting around a warm fire and a young couple, totally engrossed in each other, sitting at the bar. The barman was polishing the battered old wood of the bar that was already gleaming.

"What can I get you?" he said, putting his polishing cloth under the bar" Do you have a room for the night and a meal?"

He turned to a door behind him, opened it and called out;" Stella..." He turned back to me "She'll sort you out" he said and retrieved his cloth and then Stella stepped into my life. Straight away I knew there was something special about her. She was of flesh and blood like you and me but somehow, in some subtle way, she seemed to be made of finer stuff. There was a gentle glow of radiance around her that I had never seen around anyone else. Everyone looked round at her and smiled as she beamed at us and suddenly the room seemed brighter than before.

"We have one room left" she smiled at me "But its right at the top of the house""That's fine "I said, bedazzled by her smile, I would have said that if she had offered me a room at the top of a mountain.

"Then follow me" she said and I went willingly.

The passageway behind the bar was narrow and dark. Stella picked a lamp up and lit the way through the passage for me and up a winding staircase. The staircase passed through several floors until, at the very top of the house, just as I was beginning to tire, Stella stepped onto a landing and opened a door;" Here we are " she said " Room seven, lucky seven, best view in the house. Come on in Traveler"

I stepped into that room as if I stepped into another world. A window, on the wall opposite the door, dominated the room; for through the glass was the most beautiful starlit sky I had ever seen. I gasped in wonder. It seemed as if we were right up in the sky amidst the stars and earth was far away somewhere below.

" Sit down" said Stella and she placed a dish of exotic fruit in front of me and poured sparkling wine into a crystal glass. "Let me feed you before you float away". I ate the succulent fruit and drank the sparkling wine she gave me.

"Make a wish "she said, as I put down my glass. I closed my eyes to think. I knew that I must not waste this wish. What should I wish for? Beauty, wit or wisdom? Fame, love, or money? For my dreams to come true?

"What do you dream of?" said Stella, as if she read my mind.

A vision filled my eyes-I saw myself in a shining place where Stella held my hand; the colours there were brighter and the sounds

clearer, even the air was fresher and it smelled so sweet. My earthly self had melted clean away and I was beautiful as Stella was. We walked along a tree lined road where every tree had different blossom and the birds spoke to us in song and I understood every word of every chorus. A place where people knew my name and called out greetings to me, and a light shone ahead, a place where all the signposts pointed towards Home. This was my wish.

I turned to Stella and she smiled that radiant smile again and said;

"The signs you seek are in those stars" and then she showed me my reflection in the mirror of the sky and as I traced the patterns with my newly awakened eyes I saw the shapes of the paths I had taken on my journey, I saw the signs pointing out the way ahead, and suddenly and magically, I understood... that I was, at last, in sight of Home.

The glorious starlit sky had given way to dawn when I woke again in the room at the top of the inn. Stella was gone, and yet I felt some part of her remained with me, she had scattered stardust over me and we had become connected on the pathways of the stars, and I knew that I would see her in my dreams.

MOONLIT
Inspired by Mothr Two Moons/The Moon

As we wandered down the hillside path, night began to fall. The birds quieted after their evening song and settled down to sleep, as my dog and I went by. But we were not tired; it was cool and fresh and felt a pleasant time to travel. We had been walking a while when the dog began to whine. She drew close to me, tail tucked under her in fear. "What is it girl?" I said, reaching down to stroke her. I peered into the deepening gloom trying to see what troubled her, but could see nothing. I tried to urge her on, but she would not move, only wind herself around my legs, as if she could hide behind or between them. She whined again and then I saw, figures on the path ahead of us. But where had they come from and why was the dog so afraid? I took a step closer, nearly tripping over the dog, she yelped as I trod on her paw. The shadowy figures moved forward also, until I could see them; a girl, and old woman and a wolf. No wonder the dog whined!

"Have no fear, friend, Wolf will not touch you unless you threaten us," said the girl. The wolf sat down at her feet as if to confirm her words, but my dog still wound herself around my legs in fear.

"Where did you come from?" I asked, for I was sure the path ahead of us had been empty."From far beyond this place" she said" My name is Luna. We have been travelling for many days and my grandmother is tired. If you would be so kind as to light a fire we could rest awhile together."

My dog stayed close to me as I gathered wood but the wolf only sat beside the old woman, it's huge head on its front paws. As we sat at last before the small fire my curiosity got the better of me.

"So where are you ladies travelling to?" I asked

"I am looking for my mother" said Luna, sadly, reaching thin hands out to the fire. "Do you have a mother?" she asked me. I shrugged my shoulders; "I must have had one I suppose, but I don't remember her."

"I remember mine" she said" So strange and beautiful she was. I remember the time when I grew to fullness within her light, when I was so close to her I could hear her heartbeat and she mine, when we moved in harmony with each other, joined by a silver chord. And when I was born from within her, although the silver chord was cut, we had half each and still she shone her lovely face on me. Then there were other times, times when she hid her face and veiled herself so I could not see her or feel her love. She left me alone in the dark until I howled in pain and fear. I hated her then, because I was afraid and confused"

"Why did she leave you alone?" I asked, wondering why my mother had left me alone, for she must have done.

"At first I thought it cruel too, "she said" But as I grew older I learned three things from her. The first was that she always came back, the second, that there was a rhythm to her coming and going and the third and most important, was that there was a reason for her coming and going."

She stopped speaking and looked at me expectantly, as if I should know this reason. I did know…but I couldn't quite put it into words… I just had a sense of it…

"What reason?" I asked this was as important to me as it was to her.

"Grandmother told me." she said softly, turning her fair head towards the old woman. I turned to look at her too.

"Tell me…" I said, suddenly longing to know the answer.
The old woman sat up straighter. "To become who they are all mothers

have a lover, as yours did" she began. "And to keep her lover faithful she must lead him in the chase. So your mother leads him far across the worlds and realms where she is not always in your sight, but you can follow where she goes, she shows the way in seasons and in tides. She leaves behind a trail of magic you can follow."

Excitement filled me as she spoke; I knew that I was on the edge of understanding this mystery, this magic.

"And I must follow that trail now, for I must speak with her myself. "said Luna.

"What will you say to her?" I asked.

Luna's eyes shone in the deepening night as she spoke, illuminating the beauty in her face.

"I shall tell her the silver chord is joined again, now that I am to be a mother, as she is. My child too will be cast adrift on the waters of life, tossed through the seasons until I return and I want my child to know that I will return."

I wished I could find Luna's mother for her.

"Tell me what she looks like," I said "I may have seen her on my travels"

"She wears a gown of palest silver and her hair is dark as night and full of jewels, her eyes twinkle and shine and as she dances by she leaves a beam of sparkle in her wake"

Suddenly the dog and the wolf both rose, noses pointing to the sky. They began to howl. I looked up. I saw the full Moon shining down on us and I knew!

"There she is!" I yelled, pointing to the sky. Luna and her grandmother rose as one and we became a circle of delight....

When I awoke the following morning my strange new friends were gone. I saw a pale trace of Luna's mother as she disappeared across the sky, before her lover rose above the hill behind me. The dog woke up and nuzzled my hand. As she did I realised that I held a small jewel in it. Somehow I knew it was a moonstone, one of the Mother's jewels, one she'd left behind for me. Smiling, I tucked it into a pocket in my bag.

ANGELICA
Inspired by Sky Dancer/The Sun

I had risen early that morning and had been walking for what seemed a very long time. It was a dry dusty path I walked, and it didn't seem to be leading anywhere in particular. My legs ached, my feet were sore and I felt heavy and tired. My spirits were in much the same state as my body; tired, burnt out and fed up- as if I were trapped in a grey fog. How long could I go on like this? I asked myself. I was wandering about in a strange land and for what purpose? I didn't know I was too tired to remember. I looked ahead of me but saw only a lone tree marking a flat empty horizon. For want of something better to do I thought I may as well walk towards the tree. At least I could rest a while beneath it, and then maybe I would find the energy to think what to do to get myself out of this dark, bare, desert like place. I had been travelling for a long time and I had had many experiences along the way, but was I any closer to getting to where I was supposed to be going? And where exactly was I supposed to be going anyway?

At last I reached the tree, exhausted and heartsick, and gratefully I sank to the ground beneath its shade, resting the burning muscles of my back against its trunk. My eyes glazed over with tiredness and slowly I felt my body relax, the tension draining from me and sinking into the ground with roots of the tree. I heard bees buzzing somewhere near me, but was too comfortable to look round for them. A gentle warmth seemed to be caressing the skin of my face, and gradually I became aware of a presence all around me.

My eyes widened in surprise and I saw a radiance that lifted and lightened the whole place. From the centre of this radiance a golden haired child, in a yellow dress, beamed at me as she danced in the centre of the light. The word "who", had not travelled from my brain to my lips, when she answered me:

"I am Angelica, Child of Light, I come to show the way to travelers who get lost in dark places".
"How did you know I was lost?" I asked her
"Because you too, are a Child of Light and light can always be found in the darkness"
"Am I?" I said
"Of course!"
She laughed delightedly, pirouetting towards me and taking both my hands. I stared into her beautiful face. How could I possibly be like her? She glowed and shone with joy and life.
"

The light that illuminates me, is also in you," she said. "Reach out from the very centre of yourself- the Self that has been on many journeys and already knows the way. Let your Self shine, then you will see the true path shining clearly ahead of you, and you will dance your way along it, happy in the knowledge that it will lead you to your destination". She spun me round in her dance and I reached out to her with all my heart. And there before me I saw the path, shining and golden, rolling over the rich and fertile land before me. I stopped in my tracks, amazed at what I saw. Angelica squeezed my hand.
"It is yours, follow it" she said and I knew in my heart she was right. I reached for my bag and turned to bid her goodbye. She was gone already when I turned, but I could hear her joyful laughter like bells on the breeze. I opened the hand that she had squeezed in farewell and in my palm lay a golden coin engraved with Angelica's beautiful face. Smiling, I closed my palm around it and set off on my path, strengthened, energised and illuminated, with a song on my lips and feet that danced with joy.

THE SUMMONING
Inspired by Transformation/Last Judgement

I sat on the green hill cocooned like a chrysalis in mist. I sensed it was near to dawn, though the dog and the world still slept. I eased my green boots from my aching feet- they were well worn now with all my journeying, but the blind man had served me well by selling them to me. I scrunched my toes in the cool dewy grass. The feeling reminded me of the day I had arrived here, - on another green hillside. It seemed such a long time ago now. I pulled my bag towards me and opened it to find the music box. I played the tune and again and remembered the dog and I setting off on our adventures, I remembered too the wonderful songs of Duet. Humming to myself, I put my hand back in the bag and touched the faded petals of the Wild Rose tasting again on my tongue the sweetness of the food she gave me. I remembered the people I had met; the beautiful otherworldly women- Gypsy, Stella and Luna and their gifts of gentle wisdom. And their male counterparts- the magical Wolman, the Lord and the Poet who had guided me so well. I remembered more- I had spoken with a timeless living Statue, experienced the turning of the Wheel, fed at a magical Feast with creatures I never could have imagined. I had been tormented by dark Shadows until I faced my fears and then illuminated by the Sun and Moon. I emptied the contents of my bag onto the ground before me. The moonstone glowed softly and mirrored the mist that swirled around me. My fingers touched the strings of the harp and a pure note rang out. My spirit stirred and I leapt to my feet, the mist around me began to roll away, as if it too had heard that note that was a summoning. The dog woke suddenly, her ears pricked up and she too leapt to her feet.

As the mist drew back further I saw that we stood before an arched wooden door, in what looked like a city wall of weathered grey stone. I looked to right and left of me but both sides were still veiled by the mist. I gathered up my belongings trying to work out what to do, and as I went to close the bag I saw a golden key lying in the grass in front of me. My fingers reached for it, knowing as they did, that this key would grant me access through the door. I turned again to face the door, stepping closer as I did. I noticed that there were carvings on the door, carvings of signs that were familiar to me; signs that were summoning me to open the door. The dog nudged my hand with her nose as if to urge me on so I put the key in the lock. I turned it once, twice and thrice- at last it was unlocked. The door swung open and like a butterfly emerging from a chrysalis, I stepped through. My harp sang the note again, this time accompanied by an otherworldly choir, voices so pure and true they painted the air with vibrant colours as they rang out. I sensed the summoning becoming stronger, drawing me in to this place of light and colour, this place that summoned me because it was familiar. I walked towards the coloured lights, knowing I was coming closer and closer to discovering something some part of me already knew, some part of me that had been sleeping and must now wake up. The note rang out a third time and now the summoning was complete, at last the veil of mist was gone, my destination clear. I knew I was on the last leg of my journey, and others joined me as I walked in light and music, and our souls sang all the way home.

THE STORYTELLER
Inspired by The Reaper/The World

And so, at last, I came, along a once familiar path, to my home. Familiar faces gathered round to welcome me back, with tears and laughter shining from their eyes. I was ushered to the place of honour in the circle of my old companions. The dog too, received her fair share of pats on the back and fond greetings, as she took her place in the circle next to me. There was music and song to welcome me home and festive food and drink was passed around the circle many times. Thanks were given for my safe return and eager faces turned to me with questions on their lips; Where did you go? What did you see? What have you brought back? I laughed aloud with glee! I had tales enough to last a whole season!

It seemed a whole lifetime ago that I had set out, with my dog, not knowing what lay ahead of us. But I had walked another land, breathed different air, watched the tides of faraway seas and sat by the fires of strangers. Smiling at my companions, I emptied my bag into the circle. I opened the lid of the little music box and the tune played once more and I began to tell of my adventures. I remembered the first time I had heard the tune, when I realised that I had lost all memory, not only of who I was, but of the purpose of my journey. My audience shook their heads in wonder. "How terrifying!" they said. And wondered more when I told them that it mattered little that I did not know who I was-having no memory gave me a freedom , I had no fear of making mistakes or of plans going wrong, for I had no memory of either.

And the land I travelled to had seemed to welcome me. I painted pictures with my words of the green hills and flowing waters of this beautiful land, and saw again in my mind's eye the towns and cities I had travelled through. But my listeners grew quiet and still as I told of the characters that peopled this place and the real magic I had experienced through meeting them, and as my story poured forth I began to realise just how much I had learned on my journey, how much I had changed and grown, somehow become more complete.

Some of it had been difficult, some of it had been frightening but all had added something to the person I had been when I started out, made me stronger and steadier. A warm sense of wonder began to glow within and around me like a starry cloak.

As I neared the end of my story, one soft dark night, I cast my eyes over the gifts I had been given, all brought safely back in my bag, each reminding me of something I had learned, each a symbol of some experience, and I felt humbled and grateful for this, but I knew these gifts were for passing on.

So, as the season drew to a close I gave them away; the music box to a friend with an ear for music, the painted wagon to one who longed to travel , the green boots to one whose own were worn and down at heel, the moonstone to one who missed her mother, until at last it was all gone. For my purpose had not been to gather material things but to gather stories.

The night I gave away the last of the contents of my bag and told the last my tales, was one of joy and celebration. A child who had been but a babe when I had left hung a garland of flowers round my neck, their heady scent wafted round me as I heard a voice cry, from the other side of the circle ;

"Let's hear it for Storyteller and her companion, the dog called Faith". To thunderous applause Faith and I took a bow and left the circle, with our empty bag and our light hearts, to rest before our next journey. When our new story would begin.....

MINOR ARCANA STORIES

IGNITION
Inspired by Ace of Fire

The red haired boy sat cross legged on the ground, totally concentrated on the two sticks he rubbed together so vigorously. He would spark this fire, coax flame from the wood with his focused will. Desire burned strong within his heart. His blood pulsed with energy and warmth. He would hold this torch aloft, proving he had the skill to transform sentient fuel into translucent, living flame using only the magic within himself. The sticks grew warmer and warmer as he laboured, passionate in his determination.

A puff of smoke rose from his hands, blurring their motion… then another, acrid with the scent of scorching heat that seared his nostrils. At last a tiny flame sparked. The boy kept his sore hands moving, sweat trickling down his dirt blackened face, until the flame grew and grew and burst forth from the sticks in an orange flash. The flame swallowed the air, flared and grew, burning steadily now, pure and bright illuminating the dark day. He leapt to his feet and raised his torch in triumphant salute to the sky, then lowered it to the kindling at his feet. The flame licked the dry wood, igniting it. The wood crackled and popped as its shape and form changed. The red haired boy smiled to himself- the fire was lit, now let the magic begin

THE UNDERSTUDY
Inspired by 2 of Fire

Ivy stood at the stage door, watching her friend Ruby playing the part. Ivy mouthed the words in perfect time with Ruby, she knew them so well. As another player began a long monologue Ivy's mind began to wander. How she would love to play the part, to step on the stage and be the character she had come to know so well. But for that to happen Ruby would have to be ill or something, and Ivy wouldn't wish that on her, like most performers, Ivy was superstitious, but she was fed up with being the understudy. Every night she had to be ready and focused, and yet every night she stood by the stage door in the dark, unable to shine on the stage as she intuitively knew she could. She couldn't see a way through the frustration she felt, after all she had been willing enough to accept the job of being Ruby's understudy.

The monologue came to an end at last and Ivy returned her focus to the play, following Ruby's words and actions from the shadows right to the end of the scene. She turned away quickly as the curtain came down, hurrying away to the dressing room before the actors left the stage. She didn't feel like chatting between scenes tonight. She sat in the deserted dressing room staring at herself in the brightly lit mirror when she heard footsteps running along the corridor and someone calling her name.

"Ivy! Ivy! Get your make up on girl, Ruby's twisted her ankle..."

Unable to believe her ears and flooded with the fear that she had brought bad luck on Ruby; Ivy opened the dressing room door.

"There you are!" said the director "You've got three minutes... come on get changed!"

There was no more time to think. Within two minutes Ivy was back at the stage door. She felt sick, her mind was blank, and her mouth was dry. What if she couldn't speak? The director put his hand on her shoulder;

"Steady there girl...listen now..."

With an effort of will Ivy pulled herself together; she listened; she heard her cue and stepped out from the darkness into the light. As she spoke her first words joy flared up inside and she lit up the stage with her presence.

GOLDEN ROAD
Inspired by 3 of Fire

They say things come in threes and so they did to me; I dreamed one night of a golden road, that led I knew not where. But its warm light drew my feet towards it. But then I woke, disappointed to be back in my bed. I carried the dream with me like a talisman for days and then the second happening drove it from my mind.

The Academy where I studied was to close and my fellow students and I were to be cast out to make our own way in the world. We had been told that we had learned enough of theory and were now to go forth and use our skills. I had known for some time that this would happen but had pushed it to the back of my mind- now it was happening and it disconcerted me. I had been a happy student, reveling in my studies, but all things must change and so must I. And so I busied myself, anxiously preparing, as best I could, to move on, although I knew not where for I had made no plans.

Then one night a fellow student, of a more carefree nature than mine, in an effort to cheer me up, invited me to meet him at the Golden Gate Inn .Fearing I would not see him again I agreed to go. The rosy summer sun was setting as I arrived at the inn to find, not pies and ale as I had expected, but a feast of summer fruits and rich red wines and cordials. My eyes filled with tears at such a sight. My friend threw his arm around my shoulder.

"Come, come" he said "Don't be sad for days gone by, celebrate the fruits of those days instead and your heart will be open for those yet to come"

We ate the luscious fruits and drank the wine till we were warm and mellow and I felt my heart open to embrace life happily again.

It was late that night when we tumbled through the door of the Golden Gate Inn. The road ahead was lantern lit and golden, like the road I had dreamt of. A horse and cart stood waiting patiently, without a word we knew it waited for us. So we three set off; - my friend, the horse and I- along the golden road that I had learned led to the future.

THE WELCOME
Inspired by 4 of Fire

Annie Smith felt the unfamiliar weight of the bunch of keys in her jacket pocket. A little thrill of excitement buzzed through her- today was The Day- at last she had the keys to her own home. She had wanted this for so long, had worked so hard with this aim in mind.

Having her own space, her own independence, somewhere she could be herself. It was all she had thought of since she had first peered past the for sale sign at the Old Forge. It had everything she had dreamed of; it was old, ancient in fact, but it was beautiful and rich in character. It was a place she felt strongly that she could live and work in. It stood back a little from the winding country road just on the outskirts of a village, where there was peace and quiet but without too much isolation. It needed some work done on it, of course- she wouldn't have got it at such a good price if it had not got some faults, but it was nothing she couldn't manage, the survey had confirmed that the structure was sound.

The removal van was early and Jasmine and Tony, the friends who were to help her move, hadn't arrived. But all her boxes and bags were packed so she climbed in the van with them with hardly a backward glance. Just as they finished unloading at the other end Annie's mobile bleeped. It was a text from Jasmine saying they had broken down but would be there ASAP. Annie felt a little odd as the removal van pulled away but she shook herself inwardly and walked in to the house to start sorting out the boxes while she waited for Jasmine and Tony- at least she could unpack the coffee cups and the kettle. She was half way to the bottom of her third box in a hunt for the kettle when there was a knock at the back door. To her surprise it wasn't Jasmine and Tony at the door, it was a young girl with flame coloured hair and a cherubic toddler in her arms, accompanied by an elderly lady. The girl offered her hand to

Annie, still balancing the child on her hip.

"Hello, we are your neighbours from across the way there. I am Rosalind; this is my grandma Rosa and baby Rosie. We've come to welcome you to the village".

"Oh how nice! My name's Annie, come in, won't you? Don't mind the boxes." Annie led the trio into the kitchen.

"Have you lit your fire yet Annie?" asked the old lady.

"No, I've only just got here" said Annie, wondering if the old lady felt the cold," I don't even know if there's any fuel".

"There will be, Mary will have left the fire laid when she left, its tradition."

"Really?" said Annie, intrigued now

"Yes, it's for the welcome ceremony. To bless your house and light your first fire from the community fire, as we welcome you to our community."

"How lovely" said Annie, smiling and feeling a lovely warmth coming over her.

"Let's get it done then" said Rosa "Get the blessing tools for me Rosalind and give Annie the flame to hold"

Still with the baby on her hip Rosalind turned to do her grandmother's bidding.

"Come on Annie, we need to start outside" she said

An eagerness joined the warmth in Annie and she followed the golden haired stranger outside.

Time seemed to cease for a while as she followed her neighbours in circles around and through the house, their bell like voices singing a softly rhythmic, half familiar chant. The procession stopped before the ancient hearth and Annie knelt to light the flame from the one from the community hearth that she had been given. The neatly laid kindling sparked into life as if by magic. Delight radiated from Annie's face as she handed the community flame back to Rosa and the whole room lit up with welcome and blessing, just in time for the boisterous arrival of Jasmine and Tony and the beginning of a wonderful, impromptu, house warming party.

BALL OF FIRE
Inspired by 5 of Fire

Will listened to the voice booming over the loud speakers as Shorty checked his boxing gloves.

"And next on our bill tonight, ladies and gentlemen-the Ball of Fire himself- Big Will Allbright fights Joey the Snaaaa...ke"

The applause thundered and Will felt the adrenalin begin to pump as he skipped from foot to foot, let them roar a little louder before he made his entrance. Let the slippery Snake slither out. The roar grew louder, as he knew it would and Will danced into the ring, raising his arms above his head to greet the crowd. The roar reached a deafening crescendo as they saw the red haired fighter appear. He gazed across the ring, forgetting the crowd as he focused on his dark eyed opponent, whose oily skin was being dabbed with a white towel by his corner man. Will flexed his powerful shoulders, waiting for the bell to ring. Then it did and he was out of his corner in a flash, fists flying. The first two landed, then Joey the Snake began to do his trademark slither to stay out of Will's reach, trying to wear him out. For five rounds they danced with each other, with many of Will's punches hitting only air. Joey the Snake's slimy face weaved up and down around Will, taunting him without words. Will's temper began to simmer as sweat beaded his forehead, damn Joey! he thought. Suddenly his fist flew out and landed on Joey's jaw with a resounding crack and Joey hit the canvas. Spark out.

The bell rang and the referee raised Will's arm in victory as Joey was helped to his feet.

Back in the dressing room he stripped off his soaking clothes and stepped into the shower, satisfied with his performance - another step on the way to being champ. He walked into the bar after his shower- he had promised himself a celebratory drink if he could beat Joey the Snake. The bar was crowded and as Will stood waiting to be served a voice behind him called out;

"Hey, Ball of Fire.... Bet you couldn't put me where you put Joey the Snake"

Will turned to see a drunken lout waving his fists. He sighed, that was one of the problems, everybody wanted to pick a fight with him.

"Maybe when you're sober, mate" he answered, using all his willpower not to lash out. The lout's friends dragged him away and Will got his drink without any more trouble. He sat on a bar stool next to an old man whose broken nose and cauliflower ear showed him to be an ex-boxer.

"I s'pose you get a lot o' that, son don't you?" he said

"Yeah" said Will "I could be fighting every night if I wanted to take them all on"

"Trouble is you'd burn out pretty quick and then you'd get hurt"

"Is that what happened to you?" said Will

"No, I got out before it got that bad. Take my advice son, put your energy and the prize money you've earned to some good purpose while you've still got it, because one day you'll be outmatched, or you'll get old and that'll be your lot."

Will stared into his drink. Somehow the champion's belt seemed a little tarnished by the old man's words, and somehow less important.

REFLECTIONS OF GLORY
Inspired by 6 of Fire

It had been a long hard campaign of protest marches, petitions and politicians and all; it seemed, to no avail. At least, until Glory stepped in. I remember the first time I saw her; walking to the front of the room in her long orange dress, such a confident stride, like a steady flame burning a passage through the motley crowd. She had a radiant smile that lit up the room and her warmth and total belief in our cause revived our flagging enthusiasm. She inspired new plans to be suggested from all corners of the room.

But it was Glory who coordinated all the plans with such flair and grace- she even balanced being an inspired leader with being an iconic figurehead who attracted others to our cause, those who would not have cared if it had not been for Glory. It was the interest of these 'others' in Glory's unselfconscious beauty and magnetism that brought our campaign to a turning point. For she had attracted the attention of the local media, it was she who attracted reporters to the crucial meeting that would decide if we had won or lost.

Five of us went to the meeting with Glory, to face the committee that would make the decision. They sat, sour faced, at a long table in front of us. Then Glory tossed her abundant golden hair and began to speak.

And with wit and eloquence she set about persuading those who would destroy what should be preserved, to desist. As she demonstrated the rightness of her own personal belief that the heritage of our past is vital to our future I watched their faces begin to change. That magic glow of Glory's held them spellbound, as the five of us stood silently behind her, all with fingers crossed behind our backs. Then flashbulbs going off around us like fireworks as our spectacular victory was recorded and Glory smiled, once more, for the cameras.

But the best of all was Glory, as she led us on a celebration dance, like we were a fairy host, around the green hill we had fought to save.

BILLY RAY
Inspired by 7 of Fire

Billy Ray stood at the top of the hill looking down at the rough wooden barricade below that barred the road ahead. He had guessed this would happen; a rival faction having the same goal would try to prevent them getting there first. It was early morning and no one else was awake. Billy's comrades slept, over the brow of the hill, and the barricade appeared to be unmanned. There was something odd about this, it did not feel right to Billy Ray, some spell must have been laid to fool them. Billy stood silently, reaching out with his awareness. Satisfied that his instincts told him true, he turned and walked back to the camp. Quietly, he woke his six comrades and armed them appropriately for the coming skirmish. Before the sun had climbed to the hilltop they were ready, silence and stealth their principal weapons as they spread out to walk behind their leader .One by one they reached the summit, backlit by the sun like shining warriors of old. On a shouted word of command from Billy's lips they raised their voices in a wild chant. The barrier below burst into flames and dark shadowy figures ran towards them. Agile as a cat, Billy Ray leapt into the air, fearlessly screaming the battle cry. Light radiated from him as he raised his staff to do battle with these dark forces that would enchant his men and rob them of their victory. Valiantly they fought, until the last dark figure disappeared and the barricade was a pile of dusty ash.

Round the camp fire that night they toasted Billy Ray, and praised his name. He waved away their accolades and moved away to sit alone.

He wondered what they would say if they knew...That Billy Ray was magic, seventh son of a seventh son, with the power of knowing.... and the responsibility of that power.

THE MESSAGE
Inspired by 8 of Fire

When the phone rang I knew straight away who it was. Eight times I let it ring, but I could feel her desperation to tell me coming down the wires and I had to pick up. If I didn't, sooner or later she would ring again and I would have to hear what she had to say, good or bad.

"Hello Heather," I said

"How did you know it was me? That old witch sense of yours, I suppose". Her voice sounded upbeat, I relaxed a little.

"So what's the story then?" I asked.

"The story's moving so fast I am having a job to keep up with it! I've got the contract in my hand ready to sign and tickets to fly to the States in eight days' time."

"Wow!" I said, relief flooding through me "All obstacles out of the way then?"

"You bet! All obstacles dealt with, all delays at an end, at last I'm up and flying! Honestly, it's like someone waved a magic wand for me, I almost can't believe it"

A warm feeling flooded through me, thank the gods, it had worked!

"Oh you believe it! And enjoy every minute of it" I said

SENTINEL
Inspired by 9 of Fire

He stared into the bonfire. Deep into the red heart of it. Images from the past flickered in the flames. He poked the fire with his staff. It spat and crackled, as if in protest, coughing out hot smoke and sparks that scorched his clothes, but he was unconcerned, he had faced worse than this. He smiled to himself, remembering his first ordeal by fire, nine years ago. How he had worked and trained to summon up his courage, honing his skill with zealous discipline. How far he had come, since then. How much he had learned, how many times he had faced and conquered conflict.

And here he still stood, guard duty now, keeping the fire burning. He knew no other way to live than the warrior's way. It was second nature to him after so many years. But the years were beginning to make their mark on him now; there was a softness coming around his once taut belly, his muscles were still strong but his reaction time a touch slower. He swung the staff high and leapt into battle stance. He could still handle whatever he had to- what he had lost in speed over the years; he had gained in skill and knowledge. Not many would dare to attack him anyway- the battle scars he wore with pride, were deterrent to most. And he knew better than to be the instigator of conflict, he must be responsible for using his abilities wisely. Wisdom was as much a part of the warrior code as skill in combat. His comrades in arms respected wisdom as much as strength, for who could rely on a fool?

He turned his back to the fire and cast his eyes over the landscape, looking for signs of his comrades returning. He sensed their presence, far off as yet, and he knew that the battle was almost over. He wondered who had been sacrificed to the gods of war tonight, for there was always a price to pay for victory. He added wood to the fire, it flared high now, illuminating the night, while he stood, like a dark sentinel, ready to cauterise the wounds.

ASH
Inspired by 10 of Fire

Ash was shattered, tired out and exhausted. She had fled the city in a panic, burning up the miles in her fancy sports car until all the hassle, the hangers on and flunkies were miles behind her. She was finished with fame - ten years at the top was enough. She stared at herself in the mirror; the harsh light of the cheap motel room did her no favours. Flame red hair that had to be dyed every few weeks to cover the grey threading through it, crow's feet around the notorious emerald eyes and the blurred jawline that would become a saggy old woman's neck She had had it- her face had been her fortune and that of all the users and abusers as well- now she was finished- burnt out and old- used up and spent. She laughed bitterly- what would they do when the golden goose stopped laying eggs for them? When the vibrant flame could no longer illuminate a stage or captivate an audience? She was too tired to care. She pulled back the bed covers- one night's sleep would not be enough. She wanted to go into hibernation- buried deep somewhere and then slowly fade into obscurity until she disappeared entirely in a puff of smoke.

Early the following morning Ash sat hunched over a table in the fast food restaurant, smoking a cigarette and drinking strong coffee, hoping no one would look her way. The restaurant was almost empty and the bleary eyed night shift waitresses ignored her. She was still tired; she had slept heavily but was not refreshed. She didn't have the strength to get up and move. She didn't even have any plans, or the energy to make any.

A discarded magazine lay on the uncleared table in front of her. Idly she turned its pages as she smoked her cigarette. She reached the horoscope page, and from force of habit that she was unable to resist she looked for Sagittarius, her sign; "Time to reinvent yourself" she read, and a tiny spark came to life somewhere within..........

A year later, and fifty miles down the road from the motel two women stood talking about a third, in the post office-come-supermarket in the village of Little Oak.

"That woman does remind me of someone, I just can't think who," said the milkman's wife.

"That's Miss Ashton from Phoenix House up at the end of the village "said the postmistress as the subject of their curiosity closed the shop door behind her." She's a bit of a recluse, someone said she writes children's books, but I don't know if it's true or not."

Ash smiled as she walked up the street, running a hand through her silver hair. She was thoroughly enjoying her new role. How well it suited her!

RUBY
Inspired by Page of Fire

Shivering, Ruby crouched down by the hearth. Rubbing her frozen fingers together she blew desperately on the embers. Dangerous or not, she had to do this, her people needed it and she was the only one with a chance of succeeding- and she could, no, she was determined she would.... or all would be lost.

Then at last, a tiny flame rose out of the grey ashes. Hope flared in Ruby's eyes- the fire was not dead! Carefully she fed the tiny flame with debris she gathered from the floor of the hut until it grew and grew and glowed, hot red and orange. Then she unwound her cold limbs and stood before her fire, letting it begin to warm her from her feet upwards. As the heat crept up her legs she turned her back, let it warm the base of her spine. The flames caressed her lower back and fingers of heat circled round to her belly. A strange desire awakened in her and a smile tugged at her lips as she began to draw in the warmth that she wanted... needed, that was spiraling

higher and higher through her body. It reached her shoulders and she closed her eyes and arched her neck backwards. Her pale gold hair hung inches from the fire. But only the flame within her was ignited. It flared, burning and burning, melting her bones, liquefying her skin, until her whole shape had made a subtle shift and the Spirit of the Flame shone through her eyes and a bright golden aura surrounded her body. The fire in the hearth burned slowly down.

Ruby stood, transformed, in the centre of the room with tiny sparks still exploding from her. The light of purpose lit her face; enthusiastic plans began to create themselves in her mind. She knew that now she could change things and show her people how to survive; now she had the power to inspire them, enlighten them and enliven them with her glowing love. She strode to the door of the hut. It opened at her magical command and the dark cold night recoiled before her sparkling presence. She drew the arrow with the markings of the stag burnt into it, from the quiver on her back. She aimed her bow and with a heartfelt cry of joy sent the flaming arrow forth- to send a message to her people, so they would know that she was coming- that they had a chance.

THE COURIER
Inspired by Knight of Fire

I knew I would never hold him- he said from the beginning that he was just passing through- but I was drawn to him like a moth to a flame.

So full of Celtic charm was he, that few could resist his twinkling eyes and Irish brogue. My sister said I should stay away, he was racy and reckless-she said, and feckless as well, whatever that meant. He had a total disregard for danger and he made my dull, safe life exciting and vibrant for a while.

From the moment he roared past me on that huge gleaming motorbike of his I felt different- as though the cobwebs around me had been blown away and everything was suddenly clearer and brighter. And when he screeched to a halt fifty yards up the dusty road into town to offer me a lift I accepted without hesitation. I went for coffee with him too, when we got there, which my sister said was brazen as well as stupid. He told me his name was James Joseph McCarthy, but I could call him J.J. He worked as a courier and had driven round towns and cities all over the world on his powerful bike. As the Irish are, J.J. was a great storyteller and he held me wrapt with tales of his exploits in places far away from our sleepy town. He soon became popular amongst the locals and the landlord at the pub gave him a job as a barman on the strength of his ability to attract a crowd. It was clear from the look of satisfaction on the landlord's face that the pub profits swelled as the weeks went by, and the drinkers laughed at J.J.'s antics and came with their friends and families just to see him. He made the sun shine brighter for a lot of people that summer, but he always had a special smile and a wink for me.

Sometimes, when my sister was busy, I slipped away to meet him after his shift at the pub and we went for rides on his bike out in the surrounding countryside. He couldn't be still; he had to keep moving, always exploring and discovering. But as the summer wore on I began to notice a difference in him. There was a faraway look in his emerald eyes sometimes and I knew he was thinking about moving on. Then the day came when he smiled at me and said;

"Gotta go, girl, time to hit the open road again"

Tears sprang to my eyes- how I would miss his bright, lively company.

"Don't look so sad "he said, lifting my drooping chin with his finger, "you should try it yourself one day".

That was the best piece of advice I ever had.

MOTHERWIT
Inspired by Queen of Fire

She fed the flames with sweet applewood so they burned higher, lighting up our faces. The rich aroma filled our nostrils as we sat in a circle. She sat in the centre of us, magnificent and majestic, glowing like a ruby in her red dress.

"Can ye see, Mother? Can ye see?" piped up one of the little ones

"Are ye burning to know, boy?" She cuffed his ear but rewarded him with that shining smile we all craved. When she turned that smile on you it was like the sun shone on a bright summer day. It gave your spirit a lift. She turned her attention back to the fire.

"Watch the flames, children. See yellow, red and gold,"
"Purple and blue" whispered the little girl to her left. She handed the little girl a small piece of wood to throw on the fire.

"Take care, mind the sparks" she warned. The little girl carefully tossed her piece of wood forward, her tiny face serious in concentration. It landed as it should and as the flames licked at, catching it a fire, the child and the Mother shared a radiance that bathed us all in warmth. The warmth seemed to soften our bones. We curled like sleepy kittens round a warm hearth. Mother's voice spoke again.

"See the pictures" she whispered. And we saw pictures; exotic birds, green and flowering trees, distant, misty mountains in far off lands.... and a road. I am sure I saw a road, a starlit road. And by and by travelers appeared, as if by magic, on that road. I wondered where they travelled to or from, and if I too could go.....then Mother's hand and Mother's voice called me back, back from a long way away, to sit beside the embers again. She gathered me in her golden gaze.
"Next time you shall light the flame"

FIRE CHIEF
Inspired by King of Fire

I didn't usually lower myself to joining the ranks of the gutter press- the ambulance chasers and disaster watchers, but this was different. I had heard on the grapevine that there was something unusual here, so I followed the others to the press conference. There had been a big blaze out at the chemical plant, half the town could have died if Mike Burnley, the fire chief, hadn't got it under control.

Nothing unusual yet I know, fire chiefs are supposed to put out fires. But Mike Burnley had gained almost legendary status for his uncanny ability to control even the most raging and dangerous of fires, and subdue them to a safe level. He didn't usually speak directly to the press but the rumours about him had reached such a pitch that he had apparently decided to attempt to put the record straight.

The whisper ran through the crowd that he was about to begin. I pushed and shoved to get a better view and as I got a little nearer the front he walked on to the makeshift stage. His dazzling good looks made an immediate impression on the gathering and flash bulbs popped to left and right before he opened his mouth. He was tall, blue eyed and golden blond, and no doubt could have made a career playing heroes in Hollywood, if he had not been a fire fighter. His face looked serious as he waited for silence, clearly this man commanded respect.

"The fire at the chemical plant was brought under control by a concentrated, skilled and focused team effort" he began.

"As are all the call outs my team and I attend."

The questions began firing at him thick and fast, trying to get him to admit something, though heaven knows what they expected him to say, or what their reaction would have been if he had said that the stories about him were true and not merely wild speculation.. He was quick witted enough to turn their questions back on them, admitting nothing, but charismatic enough to keep them on his side while he refused to play their game.

I came to the conclusion that fires weren't the only thing Mike Burnley had power over. He left the stage to cheers having added nothing further of substance to his original statement and no one but me, it seems, had noticed. Rather uncanny, as I told my editor the next morning.

ONCE UPON A TIME
Inspired by Ace of Air

It was the first cold night of the winter. Crisp and clear, but biting, cold as a newly sharpened knife edge, held in winter's grip. The trees had lost their leaves and the world outside was bare and stark. It was time for the Gathering. Word had got round that there was to be entertainment. This was the season for the telling of tales. Mystery tales with hidden seeds of wisdom and magic spells wound up in the words. Tales of great love and fierce battle, heroes and giants, ancient wise ones and holy fools. And in every tale there was a truth. We all looked forward to this time, a time to forget troubles and enjoy the entertainment. Everyone was milling about, shuffling and pushing to find a seat. Mothers shushed their babies and old folks settled creaking bones. The men drifted towards the back in a huddle. Youngsters craned their necks trying to see who would be telling the tales, arguing over which was their favourite. Tonight it was a woman, a small, silver haired woman in a dress of midnight blue with a rainbow coloured chord around her waist and a blackbird on her shoulder. None of them had seen her before. Where had she come from? What tale would she tell them? An old favourite or a new one? Gradually the whispers stopped. Silence settled like a cloak upon the room as her clear eyes surveyed us. When all was still and calm she took a deep breath and began to speak..."Once upon a time...

IN BETWEEN
Inspired by 2 of Air

I closed my eyes tightly and covered my ears with my hands so I couldn't hear them. They were arguing again and they were driving me mad. For two long hours I had been trapped between them, each trying to change the others view, swinging back and forth, from black to white, like some crazy pendulum and dragging unwilling me with them. Unwilling me, who didn't want to hear their conflict, who didn't want to get involved, to have to decide for one or the other. Unwilling me, who only wanted peace and calm and quiet, becoming affected by their conflict. I didn't even know what they were arguing about. I didn't want to know. Perhaps I should have sung to drown out their angry voices- but no, I couldn't, for if I did it would reveal that I was there, hiding, and they would turn on me. I fidgeted, becoming irritable, I must get away, and to somewhere I couldn't hear them. I could not move from my hiding place, for they would see me, so I had to go in instead. Deep in the In Between it is quiet and still, no one speaks and nothing stirs, all is peace and silence. I shifted myself to the start of the secret spiral that only I knew. I let myself drift down and down, light as a feather and free as a bird, round and round. One more turn and I would be away from the voices, unable to hear their ranting and rowing, one more and I would slip into quiet and still. I would disappear into the space that is In Between, where I can listen and be and breathe.

CHIMES OF CHANGE
Inspired by 3 of Air

The cold east wind blew through the bare trees echoing her desolation, as she stood on the veranda... He was gone. The house was empty. The wind chimes that they had hung there together sang to no one. Dead leaves littered the path. Pain pierced her heart and the tears that trickled down her cold cheeks stung like a bee sting on her frozen face, as she wandered in and out of rooms that were empty without him. Part of her had known it wouldn't last, the logical part, but she couldn't think when she was around him, only feel; passion, adoration and jealousy. He had loved to make her jealous. Which she knew was cruel, but still she let him do it. He always made her aware of the shadowy others that came into their relationship, as if he liked hurting her. And then he would talk her round again, and she would forgive him, and her pain would be transformed into pleasure. She cursed herself for being taken in by his glib tongue. Why had she let herself be manipulated like that? She began to get angry- with herself and with him- it was no longer the shadowy third person that was to blame. She dashed the tears from her face. She took his photo from its frame and ripped it, once, twice, three times. She would not cry over him. She would change- get tough; follow her mind instead of her heart. In a way he had done her a favour she supposed, disappearing into thin air the way he had. The magic between them was long gone; at least now the humiliation was over too. She grabbed her coat from the rack in the hall and opened the front door. Slamming it behind her, she lifted her chin into the freshening wind.

The wind chimes sang on the veranda as she walked away.

WHERE THE FOUR WINDS MEET
Inspired by 4 of Air

Far away, beyond the furthest mountains you could see, there was a hidden place. Many tales were told about this place. It is said that only those with Bird Knowledge knew the truth of it, those who flew there by magical means to hear the wisdom of the Winds.

But at certain times of the year something extraordinary would happen to this place; the Four Winds would all blow towards it at the same time. It is at one of these times our story takes place...

Martin shouldered his back pack and swore softly- what a time of night to have to look for a shelter, he shouldn't have taken that last lift out of town. It was windy too, he hoped a storm wasn't blowing up or he was likely to be blown right off the mountain. He stood still for a moment, listening- which way should he go? The wind whipped around him pulling his clothes. He turned against the wind to a sound behind him - what was it? - Bells? He listened, there it was again- chiming, tinkling- the wind blowing something. Martin smiled and bent his head to the wind in the direction of the sound- something might mean somebody too- even a house. Tree branches grabbed his pack and leaves tangled in his hair as he struggled up the incline, but the sound kept calling him. Determinedly he followed it, pausing every now and then to listen. At last his patience was rewarded and the trees let him go. He stumbled into a clearing- the land flattened out to a gentle slope atop which was a small wooden building. Wind chimes tied onto the tumbled down porch tossed their tune into the increasing wind and a light flickered in the window.

A gust of wind from behind him hustled Martin toward the door. It blew open as he raised a hand to knock, ushered him in and slammed it behind him. The building was empty; the light was from a small lamp on a table directly ahead of him. Martin let his pack slide from his back- at least it was shelter. He settled himself to wait out the night here, legs outstretched and head resting on his pack. He closed his eyes and listened to the rising wind- or was it winds? - blowing in all directions around the little wooden hut. But it was peaceful inside, with just the lamp burning steadily and Martin laying there listening. The winds blew stronger and stronger until the door banged and the window rattled. Martin sat up with a start, staring round wildly, the lamp dimmed and Martin froze as he became aware of presences in the room. Unable to speak, his eyes strained to see. To the north of the hut was a black, shadowy blur, on the eastern wall, a haze of purple, shifting and moving. Opposite, in the west, was a pale colour, between green and grey and where Martin sat, in the south, a gentle white light hovered. Suddenly, every trace of fear left him....

He couldn't tell any more than that, he even became tongue tied when he tried to describe where the place was. All he could say was that he was a changed man.

Martin left the area soon after. He left his back pack behind but, as it only contained four things: a leaf, a feather, some old wind chimes and a small penknife, no one bothered to try and send it on to him.

But he was often spoken about when the Winds rose at certain times of the year. Eventually he became a part of local folklore, and newcomers were told of The Man who found the Place where the Four Winds Meet.

THE COUNCIL
Inspired by 5 of Air

The wind gusted through the open window, ruffling the pages of the Book of Lore as the cold hard faces of the five council members deliberated my case. I forced my gaze to the floor with an act of will. I must not let them see the stirrings of my rebellious spirit, they must not know how angry I was at having to surrender myself to them, to be disposed of as they thought fit. At the stroke of a pen I could be condemned to swinging from the oak tree outside on the end of a rope. My little band of rebels had been scattered and all I could do now was try to salvage something from the situation. I tried to gather my wits to answer the questions that I had been brought here to answer. I must answer truthfully, as the Book of Lore decreed, for it was not the Lore we rebelled against, but it was my duty to try and divert attention from those of my band who may have reached freedom.

They whispered and muttered amongst themselves, casting sidelong looks at me. Every nerve in my body taught with tension, I strained to hear what they said but could not. Panic began to edge into my mind, I could not think of coherent answers to give, and then something dawned on me. My inability to answer meant I must play for time- let them mutter all they will. I put a look of slack jawed ignorance on my face and when at last they spoke my name I did not answer. I struggled to maintain my pose of stupidity and they adjourned my case, due to my lack of response. I was thrown into a cell but at least my companions had a chance now and I had bought myself some time to think of answers.

BOAT RIDE
Inspired by 6 of Air

I stood in the trees on the clifftop as dawn rose, watching the boats in the harbour below. They looked like toys from up here, not vessels made to journey across open seas. Ah open seas! Breathing deeply, I stepped out and looked beyond the harbour, to the wide expanse where cool, deep green sea met soft, rosy sky. That was the direction for me. It was time for me to leave this embattled land, I could do no more here, could serve no further purpose. But first I must find the vessel I had been told would take me and be there ready to board it when the wind was right for sailing. I shouldered my light pack, containing only the bare necessities I had been allowed to take after my last mission, and headed down the arrow straight path that led from the cliff top into the harbour.

Scavenging sea gulls dived down squawking, to grab the scraps of fish and food as the previous night's catch was landed from the fishing boats. Hungry fishermen called to each other as they headed off for their breakfast. But it was not a fishing boat I sought, I had been told to go to an inn called The Feathers, where the party I would accompany had stayed the night. I found the inn beside the harbour master's place and as I approached it the door opened and six white robed figures emerged, I could not tell if they were men or women. I stopped in my tracks- what kind of journey would this be? As the thought crossed my mind the last of the figures turned and beckoned to me. Without hesitation I followed. We came to a alongside a large vessel. Several other travelers were waiting to board; an old woman with a small boy, a middle aged couple and an old blind man. All stood aside to allow the white robed figures to board first. They seemed to glide aboard the boat, their combined weight barely moving it as they moved silently, to line up in a v shaped line at the prow. Just as silently, the rest of us boarded the boat. Already the noise of the harbour seemed to be retreating. The one at the centre of the six figures lifted a hand as if to test the wind. As the hand lowered they all began to chant; a strange haunting sound that I knew I had never heard, but that was achingly familiar. As the chant rose the sails billowed and the boat began to move, steadily forward as the wind carried the chant towards the mouth of the harbour. The figure at the centre raised two arms and the gates of the harbour opened. The wind strengthened and we sailed through, and the wind parted the last layer of cloud to reveal a shining sun. The white robed figures became six white swans flying above the boat. The chant continued sweet and strong as we travelled on towards the sun. On and on, further and further, into the wide open sea, until the resonance of the chant deepened into song, rich and vibrant. Before my eyes a vision rose from the sea- a palace of shining crystal, a jewel set in lush greenness. Was this paradise our destination? I did not know, I only knew that struggle had been left behind me and my journey was magical one…

ESCAPE
Inspired by 7 of Air

I dare not breathe for fear of being caught. The boundary was only feet away from me but I could hear the guards approaching. My heart hammered in my chest as I tried to gather my scattered wits and think of what to say if they found me hiding here in the shadows. The plans we had made had gone awry so now I had to think on my feet. The guards drew nearer. I could hear the crunch of heavy boots on gravel and the rumble of voices. The tantalizing smell of cigarette smoke wafted towards me. An agonising tickle tormented my throat- to cough now would get me shot... But they walked by, talking already of supper and the end of their shift. Grinning at the sameness of people,

I uncurled myself from my hiding place and crept stealthily forward- the word freedom pounding as a mantra in my brain. I reached the boundary- a wall to be scaled- here I would be defenseless for several minutes but there was no other way. If I could do this maybe I could make it to the border seven miles away.

Taking a deep breath I began to climb. I was almost at the top when a shot rang out, sending me scurrying in a panic over the wall to land in a ditch on the other side, all breathe knocked out of me. Shouting voices from the prison yard reached my ringing ears.

"Fools you are- shooting at shadows- there was no one there, or they would be in a heap on the ground now".

Stunned as much by this as by my fall, I missed the reply and the voices faded away, restoring quiet normality to the night. Carefully I sat up, knowing I was not safe yet and would not be until I was far away from this place. Praying that my luck would hold I dragged my bruised and aching body out of the ditch. The night was dark and still now- the border beckoned. With one last glance behind me I was off.

CHASING THE EIGHT
Inspired by 8 of Air

She didn't think what the consequences of her action might be- if she had known surely she wouldn't have done it, she would never have done it intentionally, would she? She was a bright, intelligent girl, lively of mind and body, and had been selected as a good candidate for magical training.

It was the curiosity that often got her into trouble that was behind it all. She could not sit and wait for her Teacher as she had been told to. She had to pull aside the gauzy curtain when it fluttered invitingly. She had to approach the octagonal table and pick up the Sacred Text that rested there. And worse still, her ignorant hands had to rifle the pages, until she saw, in illuminated golden letters, the spell so secret that I dare not write it here, the spell that none but the highest Initiates must utter, the spell of Chasing the Eight.

Her blue eyes lit up. "Magic words!" she said and she began to read them aloud. As the first words issued from her lips a tension gripped the small room, the very air seemed to thicken and swirl, as she spoke. The gauzy curtain blew back and blue and white misty shapes poured through, swirling round her in figures of eight, then she stumbled in her reading and mispronounced a word. The mist rose up and tangled around her. She dropped the Sacred Text and spun round, blinded, breathless, and unable to speak; her hands groped the air around her. Curiosity turned to confusion and clarity to distortion as the mist gripped her in its ghostly grip and swirled her around.

The High Priestess had to be summoned in the end, to undo the Word she had mis- spoken and release her from eternally Chasing the Eight, but even she could not fully restore the girl's sight. Her blue eyes were forever misty after that, although it was said that all Inner paths were clear to her and she would one day be a great Seer.

THE 9TH VICTIM
Inspired by 9 of Air

The wind howled outside, the lights flickered and the radio spluttered into white noise and then silence. Something crashed to the ground outside and she jumped to her feet.

"Some safe house this is" she muttered to herself. The lights flickered again and she wondered about candles. She should look now before the lights did go out. She began to open cupboards and drawers in the huge dresser that adorned one wall of the room, feeling like a burglar she glanced over her shoulder, even though she knew there was no one there. Or did she? She shook her head impatiently, no good thinking like that, or she would scare herself witless. Of course the house was safe- that was why she was here, and no one knew except the witness protection officer. The last drawer yielded a dusty candle stub about four inches high that would have to do. The lights went out as her hand closed over her cigarette lighter. Relieved, she flicked it, once, and again, a tiny flame caught the wick and flared higher, casting shadows around the room and across the high vaulted ceiling. Shivering, she sat down in the old fashioned armchair. This was a strange house. She had seen the words Raven's Keep above the front door when she had arrived. From the outside it had looked like many other stone cottages in the area, but inside was this room with its high arched ceiling and a winding staircase leading to the shadowy upper floor. Last night she had been wakened, heart thumping with fear, by tree branches in the overgrown garden tapping on her window. Tonight she had decided to sleep downstairs. She wondered who the house had belonged to. It was a very lonely place, almost hidden at the end of a dark lane. She had told the witness protection people she would prefer somewhere quiet, but this was isolated. She wondered why it was called Raven's Keep- Wasn't raven the death bird? She shivered again. She had been cold ever since she got here. Cold and frightened. Frightened that what she had done would be found out. That those she had betrayed would come hunting for her, with knives or guns. She huddled deeper in the chair, tucking her cold hands under her armpits. She had seen their handiwork before and that was what had made her tell- the victims. Oh God the poor victims! But now she was a victim too, the ninth victim. Although no crime had been committed against her, and she had committed no crime, she was suffering and being punished as if found guilty. Tears of fear and self-pity filled her eyes. The storm raged louder outside as if it was screaming her feelings. The candles flickered as a draft blew the curtain behind her; she turned quickly in her chair to see the ghostly face of the moon haunting the dark clouds that sped across the sky. The wind rose like the voice of the banshee to a crescendo of unholy terror. Grotesque nightmare images chased across the vaulted ceiling. Panic rose in her throat,

"Hold on, hold on" she told herself, hands clasped as if in prayer and eyes tight shut. Over and over like a mantra, "Hold on till morning... morning will come... hold on......."

SURRENDER
Inspired by 10 of Air

A bitter wind blew across the battlefield. Instructions to surrender were passed down the line and a white flag was raised. From the edge of what had been no man's land, ten soldiers watched the flag in silence, waiting for a reaction from the enemy. The sergeant felt a piercing pain inside as he watched the flag - as if a sword had pierced and wounded him. The corporal listened to the stillness that hung between the warring factions, waiting for something, though he knew not what, to happen.

The keen young lance corporal, not long out of military school, felt disappointment- it was over and they had lost. The most experienced of the privates knew the time to lay down arms had come; he smiled ruefully at the defeated look in the eyes of his friend from back home, who threw his weapon down in frustration.

Amongst the three younger privates who had only recently joined the fight; one saw the sense in moving away from conflict, he longed to seek a more peaceful solution. One began to plan how he would escape capture and one stood frozen and petrified of the unknown fate that awaited him. Two more soldiers sat with their backs to the trench wall, one wishing he could soar away into the sky and not be part of all this, he had no wish to be a prisoner of war. And the last soldier whispered the words that broke the silence -

"War is over, time to make peace"

ROSA THORN
Inspired by Page of Air

As the last shadows of the night faded I saw her standing there, on the side of the mountain. Her dress was pale pink, like the dawn, shot through with silver, like her eyes, that flashed steely anger at me, detracting from the air of vulnerability about her slender figure.

"Be gone, traitor" she accused me. "Leave your dagger on the rock".

I knew there was no point trying to explain. Rosa had no intention of listening to me; she had turned her back already and covered her ears with her hands like a child, unwilling to be persuaded, unwilling to hear the truth. Reluctantly, I laid the dagger on the rock as she had told me. She turned in one swift movement and snatched it up.

"Be gone before I cut your heart out - ah but you don't have one do you? You sold it when you sold us out didn't you?" she sneered

"Rosa, I..."
"Will I scar your body with this dagger, as well as scar your soul with my curse?"

She lifted the dagger, poised to throw and hit her mark. I turned to go, my shoulders bowed with the weight of her curse. I had little choice now, for I knew she would maim me with that dagger if she could. All in the name of the Thorn family honour and I would not die for these crazy mountain people, not after what I had seen them do. But Rosa would, she loved them with all of her fierce little heart and would defend them to the death - such a pity all that energy could not be pointed towards a more peaceful cause, one more deserving of her loyalty and of her cleverness. Unwilling to abandon her, I turned for one more look but she was gone, disappeared without a trace into the barren rocky landscape that was her home.

PARTISIAN
Inspired by Knight of Air

A small crowd began to gather in the market square. Word spread quickly that he was there.

"Robin's back! Robin's back!" An air of excitement caught the people as the slim dark haired figure took up his instrument. He looked around at the gathering faces with eyes the colour of a summer sky, drawing them in effortlessly with his charisma. What would he play today? What daring would he show them this time? Anticipation built and Robin smiled slowly, white teeth gleaming through his ragged beard. He blew a note from the flute effortlessly and the crowd sighed- at last! The crowd parted and three scruffy individuals appeared from their midst to surround Robin and the tune began. Rattle and drum and a second flute accompanied Robin's song. The crowd began to sway and clap in time as he sang the words; the words that cheered them, the thinly disguised lyrics, that to the soldiers of the ruling regime sounded like some folk ditty, that craftily reminded them of the possibility of freedom from oppression- the words that incited them to remember who they were and the power they had once had.

Robin didn't care if the soldiers understood the words today- this crowd was big enough for him and his fellow musicians to get lost in. So he increased the volume of his singing, he played to the crowd, rousing them to a defiant pitch. The crowd loved Robin, brave Robin, the freedom fighter- who dared to defy the authorities with his protest songs. Robin, who carried messages to the resistance movement in the tunes he played and flirted with danger for his own ideals and all their sakes.

The tune reached its crescendo and spiraled down to the last beat as another message began to pass through the stomping, chanting crowd;"Soldiers- three platoons marching this way- tell Robin, danger! - tell Robin..."

A heavily armed sergeant began pushing through the crowd. "What's going on here? Disperse or be shot".

The crowd pushed tight around him- pushing and squeezing, till he could hardly move or breathe...

At last he got to the centre of the crowd and could lift his gun- but there was no one there, nothing... just... space...as he circled warily and signalled his companions, the crowd too melted away.

And Robin and his ragged band? They had run like the wind, vanished into thin air.....

But they would be back.

MOUNTAIN SHRINE
Inspired by Queen of Air

Relishing the pain in my body that stopped me from thinking I clawed my way up the mountain. Stretching arms and legs to the point where muscles screamed and lungs worked harder than ever up and up I went until at last I reached the ledge. Scrambling over the hard stone edge I collapsed in a, heap panting with exhaustion. Eventually my breathing slowed and I looked around me.

A silvery mist drifted in tendrils around the ledge, softening the light. The air was very still and I began to remember what I had been told about this mountain. It was said to be a sacred place of the ancients, there was supposed to be a shrine up here, a place where otherworldly beings came to commune with those who sought the truth. Was this what my climbing holiday was all about- a search for truth? Or was it that I had just needed to get away somewhere I could forget all my sorrows? I didn't know, or care, now that I was high on the mountain, away from everything. I peered through the mist looking for signs of a shrine, just out curiosity. What would I say to the otherworldly beings if I found their shrine? I mused, and what would they say to me?

"Are you there, ancient otherworldly beings? If you are show yourselves to me" I said, half mockingly.

"We always show ourselves to those who would truly know us" said a voice behind me.

I scrambled to my feet, my eyes searching the mist for the source of the voice. My breath caught in my throat as a grainy image began to take shape and form in front of me.

"So, would you truly know us, Jane?" It was a woman's voice, soft and bell like.

"Yes I would know you" I said, eyes straining to see her through the mist. The woman stepped forward, raising a slim graceful hand as she did to part the mist like a curtain. She wore a shimmering dress of blue and grey, a cloak of soft yellow light seemed to float around her shoulders. Her hair was blue black and her skin pure white. Piercing blue eyes gazed at me from behind a fan of multi coloured feathers.

"So few come these days Jane, and those who do come in sorrow and desperation. And it is only when they have enough belief to cry out to us, as you did, that we may answer them."

"Who are you?" I managed to say

"I am one of an ancient race who walked the same lands as your people many centuries ago- when those of your kind believed in magic- we were friends and allies then. It was my race that forged the sword your true born king pulled from the stone. But since his last battle your kind have turned away from us, the spirits of the land, to strange gods whose priests cast us as demons or figments of the imagination. So much so that now we move in separate dimensions. You sorrow because your people have forgotten how to access the ancient wisdom we hold, and we sorrow that your unbelief sends us and our knowledge fading into distant realms".

"I can see you now "I said, feeling her sadness in my own breast and wishing I could ease it. My petty troubles seemed like nothing now.

Her face lit up in a smile, radiating a sparkling clarity.

"So you can, Jane, and as your belief is strengthened so am I, according to the law of magic. And as you ease my sorrow Jane, so I will ease yours. "She lifted the fan of feathers high into the sparkling air and spoke a word in a tongue I did not understand and then she was gone. I stood awhile, hoping she might come back but then I realised it didn't matter, I knew where to find her now.

I followed a light and easy path back down the mountain, listening to birdsong as I went- a slightly different person than the one who had climbed up.

JACK DOVE
Inspired by King of Air

It was early morning, as I wound my way up the twisting path that climbed the purple, heather clad hill the faint touch of yellow among the grey clouds in the wide sky beyond, hinted at a clear day to come. Gratefully, I leaned on my stick, pausing to look out over the misty lands below as I rose higher up the slope.

As I stood in the quiet stillness a hawk flew overhead screeching a war cry at prey only he could see. This brought to mind the reason for my climb. To see the elusive Jack Dove and ask his advice. I had been told that the best way was to call very early, as Jack rose with the birds, and would be off somewhere in the nature reserve doing his conservation work and I could wander about all day and not find him. As I climbed a little further I could see the cottage I had been told he lived in, nestling into the side of the hill. If I had not been told it was there I would have missed it, so well was it camouflaged. I paused again to gather my thoughts. What a magnificent view he had from here.

As the morning mist cleared a gentle sweep of rolling landscape was revealed. Fields of wildflowers and grass stretching for miles ahead to a distant forest; it was if the cities and towns did not exist. I walked up the overgrown path that led to the cottage. Was he even here? I wondered. There were no signs of life. These thoughts had barely crossed my mind when a voice behind me said;

"Are you looking for me?"
"You're Jack Dove?" I said.
"Who wants to know?" he countered.

He was younger than I had expected. Although his black hair had threads of silver his face was unlined and he carried no excess weight.

His grey eyes considered me calmly as he waited for me to answer. Equally calmly I told him who I was and who had sent me. Then I told him of my dilemma. He listened silently throughout. Then, as I faltered to a stuttering halt he began to speak.

"I can't really tell you what to do "he said "I could outline the options and possible actions you could take, but that won't help because you already know them"

"But you could give me your opinion" I said, my heart sinking at the thought that he would not help me.

"What kind of opinion could I have, son? I live way up here with the birds, miles from the city and its politics. I am not involved with this and have no wish to be"

I stared at him in confusion, how could he stick his head in the clouds like this?

"But you won the Nobel peace prize; don't you care anymore what happens to the world?"

His eyes flashed at me in anger; "I care not for the quarrels of greedy men," he snarled, "Let them destroy each other if they will, the world will be well rid of them. I have better things to do." His face and voice softened" One piece of advice then, "I waited, not daring to provoke him again.

"Distance yourself and get a clear perspective on this, then the action you must take will come clear to your own mind".

He turned away and disappeared into the cottage like a puff of smoke. Clearly dismissed, I walked back down the hill, leaving Jack Dove in peace, turning over in my mind the wisdom of his word

THE MAGIC POTION
Inspired by Ace of Water

An ancient prophecy foretold the birth of a special child- a child from a secret place that many seek but few find- a child who would bring the People love, and joy and peace. And now the stars aligned in the sacred pattern and the Seers said the time drew near. The People watched and waited. They waited for the Flower Bride to sally forth and choose her King. They made heartfelt prayers and offerings for fertility. They watched the Rite of the Loving Cup and raised their own vessels in salute, hoping from the bottom of their hearts that the Bride would become the Mother, for to them children were a blessing and a wealth beyond all other. They were glad and excited to hunt with the King, to serve the Bride delicious delicacies while her belly swelled she watched the sun and moon make circles in the sky.

At last the day came when the prophecy came true and she was born, a golden rosy babe, signed by a rainbow shimmering above the southern hills, that the Seers said was the Rainbow Path from the Otherworld. The People all rejoiced and gifted blessings on the little girl.

Brightly flowered garlands were hung throughout the Land and songs and stories woven in her name.

The Mother smiled with deep contentment as the baby's tiny rosebud mouth found the soft full breast she offered. Then she sucked and liquid love came pouring into her- a magic potion that would fill her every want and need.

THE KISS
Inspired by 2 of Water

"Meet me down by the stream" he had said," We'll sit there under the willow, dabble our feet in the babbling water". When Ma said I could go out I didn't need telling twice. I ran down the path, laughter bubbling up inside me. I kicked my shoes and socks off as I ran. He was there already. I could feel him, waiting there for me to come and I knew he could feel me too. Ever since we met we had been able to feel each other's feelings - that's how I knew that he was special. I didn't have to tell him how I felt, he knew. Ma said we were like the sun and the moon in the old stories- who fell in love and gave birth to the stars. The sun shone above us today, I saw it sparkling on the stream as I reached the willow and it shone from his eyes as he parted the graceful branches to invite me in. Willingly I went and sat beside him, we leant against the tree, fingers entwined. But he could not sit still, I felt the tension of a wanting in the heat of his skin and the rhythm of his breathe. I did not need to ask him what this wanting was. I knew why he had asked me here, the tension gripped me too, for I was young and shy. But I too, had dreamed of this moment- the moment that would set the seal on our union. I turned to face him and as I moved the stream's cool water splashed my toes- I giggled in surprise and met his smiling eyes. My shyness gone I reached for him. His hands caressed my face, cupping my chin in his hands, he drew me close to him, so close that our eyes saw nothing but each other and we could feel each other's breathe. And then he touched his mouth to mine and I heard and felt his promise without words; for we were sun and moon no more, but one- one light, one being, one kiss.

JOY
Inspired by 3 of Water

"I'm not opening the bubbly till the Aunts get here" said Caroline, snatching the bottle from her husband and stowing it under the table.

"Ok, love" he said, shrugging his shoulders. Brian had learned that it was best to agree with Caroline at family occasions and the party for their new daughter's Naming Day was no different. If she wanted her Aunts, fondly described as the three witches, to be there for the toast, then that was fine by him. He would make do with beer until they arrived.

The Aunts weren't really aunts at all actually, he mused. They weren't related to each other or to Caroline, not by blood anyway. They were, in fact, friends of her mother who had taken care of her after her mother died, and were more to her than any flesh and blood family, she had said.

Brian spotted his own mother across the room hovering over the baby's pram. He wondered how she would react to the aunts. He had already had a hard time explaining that they were having a Naming Day instead of a christening because Caroline would not promise to bring her daughter up as a Christian as she was not one herself and neither was Brian. Brian himself didn't care what they called it- as long as he could celebrate his little girl with his family and friends around him he was happy. Brian had had another beer or two while his mother still cooed over the baby, when the doors to the hall were flung open and in strode the Aunts, looking as flamboyant and colourful as ever, but to Brian's relief, not particularly witchy. Well, no broomsticks in evidence anyway. Brian's mother, in her pale suit, was engulfed as the three women surrounded the pram and was left trailing in their wake when Caroline triumphantly carried the tiny child to the table where the champagne and the cake took pride of place. The cork was popped and glasses filled as Brian's sister pushed him through the crowd to Caroline's side, hurriedly he grabbed a glass and raised it. Tears of happiness filled his eyes as his daughter was welcomed into their lives and as he looked across at the Aunts it seemed, for a moment, as if they all merged into one smiling, shining figure. He blinked and looked down at the baby; little Joy smiled up at him from her mother's arms and he felt complete.

PARTY MOOD
Inspired by 4 of Water

Today is my birthday, and for the first time in my life I don't want to go to my own party. I wish they hadn't bothered. I don't want the banner with 40 on it that'll be emblazoned across the bar telling every living soul who comes in the pub how old I am. I think I'll have a glass of wine before I get ready, I'll have to try and put a face on it and the wine might help. I hope I don't get all the "Life begins at forty" stuff. The only thing I can see beginning is wrinkles. (God, this wine is sour!) I can already see crow's feet round my eyes and my chin is not as firm as it was. Forty is the beginning of middle age. Middle age! What a terrible prospect! (I think I'll have another glass of wine - at least sour suits my mood!). Grey hair (I've got some of those already, but I had streaks put in so they don't show), false teeth and everything sagging, (my bum isn't where it was five years ago). And nobody looks at middle aged women - they don't become distinguished, like middle aged men, they just become invisible, like ghosts. That is true; I read it in a magazine! Oh, how sad is that? - I even sound middle aged - what's happening to me? Time for another glass - might as well drown my sorrows, whoops, spilled some.

Mind you, invisible might not be such a bad thing. It could even be an advantage. No one would notice that I've got wine down my dress. I could go out with no make-up on and wear what I like without worrying if it is in fashion. I read a poem once about a woman wearing a red hat and a purple dress. I could go where I like, instead of going where the in crowd go - that would actually be a relief - the pubs and clubs it's fashionable to be seen in are actually a bit loud for me and if I'm being honest - some of the music is dreadful. If I was invisible I could do all sorts of things, I suppose. I could do scandalous things if I wanted to - all though these days it would have to be something pretty extreme to be scandalous. I could do eccentric things though. People expect middle aged women to be a bit nutty don't they? It has a kind of charm to it and it would be fun. I've always tried to conform and fit in and it never really worked somehow - perhaps I would be happier not conforming - this wine is beginning to confuse me. Still being happier feels like a good idea - worth raising a glass to! (I hope I'm not becoming a middle aged drunk) I'd better get myself off to this party!

RAIN ON THE RIVER
Inspired by 5 of Water

It was a damp, misty morning as she headed down the hill towards the river. Fine rain began to wet her hair and trickle down the back of her neck. It seeped through her thin shoes as she walked. But she didn't seem to care how wet she got, or bother to wipe the tears from her face. The streets were empty but the world seemed to weep with her, the wind began to rise, it's voice making a strange keening noise, the trees that lined the road sagging with the weight of the water and swaying as if in sympathy, the unremembered joy of sunlight like a distant dream. She was soaked by the time she reached the bridge and the rain came down harder from the silver grey clouds as she leaned over the parapet, the fat, leaden drops making eddies and whirls in the green water.

She raised her face, crying out in anguish to the sky as the merciless rain beat down on her;

"Wash me clean... wash me away..."

On a sob, she raised her arm and with all her strength, she threw something into the river. She paused, head bowed, until it landed with a splash and sunk, then she disappeared into the mist on the other side of the bridge, as five tiny white blossoms flowed under it and were carried down river by the current.

I REMEMBER
Inspired by 6 of Water

I remember far, far back. I remember my past, all the days and seasons of my life, right back to infanthood. I remember being in my mother's womb and pushing my way out. And I remember the time before that. I remember when the world was young and fair and free, and the Wise Ones lived alongside us, sharing their wisdom and their magic with us. I remember the stories, charms, rhymes and songs that I learned at my grandmother's knee. I remember when the door to the Otherworld was always open and we could walk to and fro freely and we all lived in peace and balance and harmony. I remember too when we came to that crossroads in life, very much like the one you are standing at now. I looked back over my shoulder, knowing that my time of idyll was over, filling my eyes with precious sights to take forward with me, filling my ears with the sounds of home, knowing that the past was over and I stood in the present looking towards a misty future. To give myself heart as I stood on this threshold, I sang the songs we sang around the fire, the songs that told how my people lived and learned, loved and lost. If I sing them to you maybe they will strike a chord in your soul, remind you of where you have come from and who you really are. Maybe the songs you grew up with will guide your feet as you step forward into your future. And if your memories make you sad maybe the singing of them will release your pain and set you free to live your future in peace. Some tears flowed as I sang on my journey, but they were healing tears and I give thanks, often, for the good things I remember.

THE GIFT
Inspired by 7 of Water

I stared out of the window at the Moon. She was waning, going into hiding. Hiding from me when I needed light. Veiling herself with mystery when I needed clarity. Leaving me alone in the dark to make my choice.

Sighing, I sipped my herbal tea, inhaling its subtle fragrance. Really there was no choice- not if I was to be happy at last. I could no longer wear the mask I had worn for so many years, no longer pretend to be someone I was not. But I had worn it for so long I did not know if I could even recognize the real me. Who am I? I asked myself. I knew how he saw me- quiet, calm, sensible. That wasn't the real me. The real me knew that I had a something to share with the world. That was what had brought me to this point - the gift I had discovered, quite by accident that I had been blessed with. The gift that I knew could change lives. The gift that I had no right to keep to myself and that I could no longer ignore the gift he would deride and despise. Emotion swelled within me like a tidal wave, building and building ready to burst through. And there I sat, trying to choose a course of action while I still could, before confusion overwhelmed me. I had woven such a tangled web around myself I needed help to find my way through the labyrinth to the true heart of me. Why had I done such a stupid thing? I wondered. Well I suppose the truth is I thought he would not want me as I really am, so I made myself what I thought he wanted and now neither of us is happy. I could carry on the facade and try to wield my gift without him knowing- but this would feel like I was dishonouring it. I could tell him straight that I wanted to quit my job and work as a healer but I knew he would laugh in my face, for he believed such things were mumbo jumbo. I stared again at the waning Moon - my time was running out. I watched the seven sisters dancing in the night sky till nearly dawn and then, at last, somehow, I knew my fate. I could not let him turn my dreams to dust. I would end the relationship and start again, as myself, doing what made me happy, doing what I was meant to.

FISHERMAN'S FAREWELL
Inspired by 8 of Water

I woke up with the sour taste of last night's wine in my mouth. I stumbled to the sink and stood at the kitchen window with a glass of water to wash the furry coating off my tongue. It was just after dawn and the sky was still pink and misty- a new day and a new beginning for me too. Today I was beginning a journey. Last night I had made up my mind- I had even told my brothers what I was going to do- after I had had a few, of course (that stage you get to when the truth just comes out). So there was no going back. Not that I wanted to go back because I didn't. It just didn't feel right anymore. Once, going into the family fishing business had seemed exciting, and the money in my pockets felt like riches. But lately I had sickened of the sameness of it all, and longed to be far from greedy, screeching seagulls, without the stench of fish in my hair and in my clothes. They had laughed at me last night, saying that I would be back when winter came, but I knew I wouldn't. I didn't know where my journey would take me, I didn't need to know, just a packed bag and a ticket for the ferry to the mainland was enough for now. By the time I was ready to go they were all up, bleary eyed and groaning with hangovers.

"Where are you off to, kid? asked my brother Tom, noticing the bag by the kitchen door. I felt a touch of sadness as I looked at Tom, he was my favourite brother and I would miss him.

"Off to seek his fortune" said Billy, the oldest of us, challenging me with his stare.

"Don't be a fool boy, there nothing' out there that you ain't already got here" said Tom

"There's a whole world out there, Tom" I said "and I need to see it and experience it for myself"

"Make him a cup of coffee Billy, he's still drunk" said Tom, turning away in disgust.

Anger bubbled up in me and I snatched up my bag and stormed out the door, slamming it behind me.

My temper had cooled by the time I reached the docks. I was sorry for the way I had stormed out. I knew my brothers did not wish me ill. But I also knew that I must make my way without them, find a life of my own, and not just keep swimming around in the little pool of our family, and sailing out and back on the same tides.

The ferry chugged into the harbour and I boarded with the few other travelers. I went straight up on deck, eager to be out to sea, as I stood at the rail I heard voices shouting on the dock. It was my brothers- all seven of them, shouting and waving like a bunch of drunken sailors. I shouted back and raised my hand in farewell, then turned my face into the fresh sea breeze.

THE WATERFALL
Inspired by 9 of Water

I followed the stream this sunny afternoon. My time was my own for a while; my jobs done and my house sparkling. It meandered across the meadow and into a little copse of trees and there, where the land dipped sharply a waterfall sang merrily as it tumbled into a pool below and out beyond. Enchanted, I scrambled down the steep bank to watch the water as it fell. I stood mesmerised and gradually I became aware of a being that gazed back at me from the centre of the rippling rainbow colours that clothed her. She spoke to me;

"Greetings, Walker of the Land. What brings you to the Waterfall?"

"I don't know..." I stuttered, completely overawed. "I just followed the stream...I love water you see, I have always been drawn to it..." I fell silent, feeling foolish now. But she laughed with delight.

"Then Water Lover, go with the blessing of the water spirits and follow your stream" she said. Many other voices joined hers in bubbling laughter and droplets of water splashed me. As the droplets touched me I felt myself bubbling with laughter and happiness as if her magic touched me with a very special blessing.

I never found that waterfall again but the magic of the blessing stayed with me.

SEA OF DREAMS
Inspired by 10 of Water

The sun shone benignly in the sky as we made our barefoot way across the beach, my bridesmaids and I. A choir of seabirds sang the music of the waves as I made my way towards my love- one hand holding the bouquet of roses he had given me and the other holding my floaty white dress, so it did not trail in the sand. I heard the littlest of the bridesmaids giggle behind me as her tiny toes sunk into the golden grains. Slowly we walked to the circle of shells he had lain down for me and I stood beside him at the seaweed covered rocks that served as an altar. He lifted the gauzy veil from my face and his dark pirate's eyes looked into mine at last. He smiled that tender smile at me and I knew our love was true and this was right. My heart sang in time with the tide and I felt his sailor's soul join mine in song. We held hands and said our vows to a priest with serene blue eyes and a silvery robe. Jeweled rings slipped on our fingers as he pronounced us wed. We sipped from an ancient loving cup he blessed upon his salty altar, and kissed to seal our vows. We turned as one to face our friends and families and felt their love and joy wash over us.

We partied there until the tide turned and the setting sun painted sea and sky deep ruby red. I tossed my brides bouquet into my blushing sister's hands. Teary goodbyes were said, they wished us well and waved, and then we were alone. Us two, now one, at last alone.

We floated, hearts full, that night, on a sea of dreams, intoxicated with emotion and drunk on love, to the blissful land of Happy Ever After.

THE MIRROR
Inspired by Page of Water

Marie bought the mirror in a junk shop to cover a patch of discoloured wallpaper in her new flat. It was the unusual blue/ green colour of its frame resting on a high dusty shelf that drew her artistic eye. She did not bother to look at the glass before she decided to buy it, just handed over her money and waited for the assistant to wrap it in layers of paper to protect it on the way home. Excited about her purchase, she set off through the rainy city streets to hang it on her wall. By the time she got home she was humming happily to herself, and shedding her wet coat, she began to unwrap the mirror. She ran her hand over the smooth painted surface of the frame, a thrill of pleasure buzzing through her. Smiling to herself and shaking her head, she wondered why she felt so excited about it; it was only an old mirror. The glass was misty, she turned away looking for a soft cloth to clean it with before she hung it. When she came back the mist cleared from the glass but it did not reflect the ceiling of her room as it should have done, resting on her table as it was. The surface seemed to be rippling, like water. Puzzled, and wondering if it was a trick of the light or a fault in the glass Marie lifted the mirror and propped it up so she could see into it properly. The ripples changed direction, moving out from the centre. She could see colours, muted at first, then growing brighter; pale blue, green, mauve and pink. The colours swirled, like water in a pool, and became a face.

It was a child's face, a little girl; small delicate features, wispy fair hair and huge blue/green eyes. She was sitting by a pool, trailing a tiny hand in the water. She looked up suddenly, as if she had sensed another presence and a flood of feeling washed over Marie; she knew this child, she knew her wishes and her dreams, her hopes and her fears. She could feel the child's feelings as if they were her own. The child looked into her eyes and smiled gently. Something unspoken passed between the two of them. Then, playfully, she splashed the water on her fingers towards Marie and the colours rippled across the mirror again. When the colours cleared the child was gone and Marie was left gazing at her own face, into her own eyes, that now held a knowledge in them that had not been there before.

BLUE APPLES
Inspired by Knight of Water

Blue had lived all his life on the barge, riding up and down the canals, through the lock gates time and time again. He had a good life; lots of friends along the waterways, a girl in every village on the way, but lately he had felt the narrowness. The narrowness of the boat, the narrowness of the canal, the narrowness of his life. He began to have dreams about wide open seas and skies, where he floated somewhere between the two. He began to talk of leaving. His friends chided him gently;

"Off to seek your fortune, Blue? In your dreams!" .they said

He took it all in good part because he knew he was a dreamer, but it wasn't fortune that Blue was planning to seek, he wasn't quite sure what it was as yet, but it wasn't money. He felt the need to widen his horizons, broaden his experience, live a little. Then one night he had a dream that changed his life. He dreamt of walking across a wide, golden plain towards the setting sun. As he walked he became aware that he was thirsty. As the sensation of thirst came into his awareness he saw ahead of him a well, with a small metal drinking cup placed by the side of it. Without hesitation he reached for the cup and took a sip. As the liquid cooled his tongue and quenched his thirst he saw that he stood in an orchard. Apple trees laden with fruit gathered round the well, but these were not ordinary apple trees, for their silvery branches bore fruit that was blue, the blue of sea and sky. Blue reached out to pluck an apple, held it in his hand and watched it fall in half.

In the centre lay a seed and round it in the pattern of a star there were four tiny images. Blue's barge, free from its moorings, floating in the sea, a fish leaping above waves, a setting sun and a blue heart.

The next day he sold his barge and all its contents, taking only the bare

necessities with him, and headed west
.

LILY
Inspired by Queen of Water

I always think of Lily when I return to my childhood home by the sea. She said she was drawn to live by water because she had the soul of a mermaid. Lily was always saying things like that and I believed every word of it. Mother said Lily was just eccentric, with her long floaty skirts and that hippy talk about souls, but there was far more depth to her than Mother saw, and I was, and still am to this day, very happy that Lily rented Rock Cottage that summer and became my friend.

Rock Cottage, as its name suggested, was perched on the rocks right above the beach and the first time I saw Lily I thought she was a mermaid; perched on a rock singing a strange lilting song. I was so startled I dropped my bucket of crabs. She stopped singing and turned her turquoise eyes on me. She smiled and instantly we were friends. I clambered up the rocks and she gave me a glass of lemonade made from real lemons and we sipped companionably looking out to sea.

She told me she had been singing to the seals that lived around our part of the coast and how last summer she had travelled to a different sea to swim with the dolphins. She told me how she had worshiped a river goddess in a wild place far away to the west one time, and spoken with a sacred salmon in a magic pool beneath a hazel tree.

Lily filled me like a vessel that summer, with dreams and visions, of lost cities beneath the oceans and the treasures of the deep.

Waves of imaginary heroines and otherworldly creatures joined us as we walked along the shore paddling our feet in the shallows. I sought her company when childhood hurts afflicted me and her soothing voice calmed me. Gently and with care, she taught me how to feel the tides within myself and flow with them. She understood my moods and needs and dreams more than any other and I know she took great pleasure in my company, as we collected shells or swam together in the deep cool water.

Together we explored the caves below the cliffs and spoke of smugglers and secret passages, we felt the ghosts of those who had once walked these hidden ways on dark nights, and hurried back along the beach before sunset, laughing at ourselves.

And so we drifted through the long warm days, rippling with happiness. Until a cool breeze blew in and Mother spoke of school and staying home.

Then the tide of summer turned, as I had learned to know it would, and lovely Lily sailed away for some place I never knew, taking a little piece of my heart with her.

MAN OF THE SEA
Inspired by King of Water

I saw the stranger, standing tall on the deck of the boat as it drew in to the shore. Closer and closer it came until sea green eyes of fathomless depth stared into mine.
He stepped lightly from deck to jetty in one fluid movement, his eyes still locked on mine as if he knew me. He stood before me smiling gently; "I'll be in the Sailor's Arms when I've unloaded my cargo" he said. He walked away, his long tangled hair and graceful flowing gait drawing the eyes of the harbour folk as he passed by.

Shocked and confused, I hurried away from the harbour, back to hide in my house, high on the cliff top. I would not go to the Sailor's Arms to meet a stranger, I told myself. But my heart knew I would- this man of the sea had a pull on me as strong as the tide. I knew not why this was; I had always been warned of sailors with girls in every port taking ship when the tide turned leaving a broken heart behind. Everyone knew that the Lady of the Sea did not give up her sailors for any mortal woman to keep.

But still I went that night to the Sailor's Arms, drawn to him like a wave to the shore. My fears were washed away as his hand took mine and I felt the kindness in him calming me. He held a cup to my lips and I drank the brew he offered and felt its warmth kiss my throat and spread through my veins like a river running, soothing and relaxing me.

His voice caressed me with words I needed to hear- deep wisdom and guidance that took me beyond where I was to a magical, mystical world beneath the waves; a place full of wonders to explore. For many moons we voyaged there, then slowly, slowly I drifted back to my conscious self.

The stranger was gone, as I knew he would be; sailed with the morning tide. But I had no regrets; I had dived the hidden depths with him and discovered priceless treasures.

FOREST GATE
Inspired by Ace of Earth

I stand before a gate. Not an ordinary gate, like the one at the bottom of your garden. This gate is magical, it is made of woven leaves, vines and flowers. This gate is rooted deep into the ground. It has grown from seeds buried under the earth and been nurtured by the miracles of nature. Its posts are living, growing trees with branches that reach for the sky. This gate is special. I reach out to touch it, enjoying its greenness. I move nearer to smell the flowers, noticing tiny buds just beginning to open behind the bigger blooms. As I step forward, the flowers seem to bow their pretty heads, the vines and leaves move slowly and gracefully apart, allowing me... inviting me... to step through...... this Gate is open.

DAISY, DAISY
Inspired by 2 of Earth

Daisy took off her shoes once she was out of sight of the road and walked barefoot into the woods. One foot after the other luxuriating in the touch of the cool damp earth. She laughed to herself at what her city friends would say if they could see her now; Daisy Atkins, up and coming restaurateur walking barefoot in the woods. What they didn't know was that the Daisy they knew remained back on the road in the smart car she drove. Here, in these woods she was someone different altogether, here she was the Daisy who knew all the trees by name and most of the herbs as well. She sighed to herself as she wandered along the path. If only she could spend more of her time here. She loved to be so close to nature, away from the harsh concrete of the city.

Out here you could breathe fresh and green instead of stale and smoky. Maybe she should sell up her restaurant and buy a place out here instead. The trouble was, it was right off the beaten track and she wouldn't pick up any passing trade, which contributed a considerable amount to her till every week in the city. Then again, she could go for the exclusive market, advertising the place as a country hideaway. But that was a luxury she could not yet afford. Maybe she should stay where she was, at least she was doing well and she did love the buzz of the city. Sitting down between two large exposed roots of an old oak tree she took a coin from her pocket and considered tossing it. She looked up into the branches of the tree -" Heads and I become Daisy-in-the-woods" she said, out loud. "Tails and I stay Daisy-in-the-city". She tossed the coin high into the air and it landed in a clump of stinging nettles.

"Very helpful" said Daisy. She leaned back and rested her spine against the trunk of the tree, still thinking about the two possible Daisies'. A thought came to mind as she sat there, in between the roots; the tree roots were an upside down version of the branches above her, with the trunk connecting the two. The work she did was her trunk- where ever she was she would be cooking - the branches and the roots were like the two different directions she could grow in. Something nagged at the back of her mind for a minute then burst out of her mouth.

"But the two directions are combined by the trunk - the secret of cooking is the combination of ingredients - I need to combine the two daisies!" Forgetting entirely about the coin she had tossed Daisy headed, with renewed vigour, back to her car, where there was a pen and paper, so she could begin to write down the recipe for her new life.

THE BUILDERS
Inspired by 3 of Earth

The word went round amongst the Forest Folk that a temple was to be constructed in a grove in the heart of the Forest. All that it was to be. Annie Birch knew it couldn't possibly be her. She wouldn't have any idea how to build a temple; she was only learning to be a wise woman. One morning as she wandered through the Forest gathering herbs she heard voices ahead of her. Annie stopped in her tracks and stood silent, listening.

"We will meet here at dusk and the Temple will be complete by dawn" said a voice vaguely familiar to Annie, but one she could not place- surely too light to be Mark the mason, it sounded like a girl.

"Till dawn then" said a second voice, with a deeper note that Annie thought she knew… was it Robert the master carpenter?

There was no third voice only the sound of a single musical note and then the sounds of people moving off through the Forest in different directions. Annie was puzzled, and could not work out what was going on. She decided to come back in the Forest before dusk and conceal herself amongst the trees to see just exactly what would happen.

So she curled herself, small and inconspicuous amongst the trees and bushes and she watched as the three approached, again from different directions. First to step into the grove was Grace Willow, Annie was confused- Grace was a dancer, not a builder, what could she be doing here? Before she could think of the answer another unexpected face appeared- not Robert the carpenter but Joel Lark, the singer. Then from the third direction stepped Leaf Brown the piper, a clear high note coming forth from his pipe in greeting.

Annie grew more curious, these people could not build a temple, surely? They had no tools and were artists of a different kind all together. Then Leaf took the pipe from his lips and called out;

"Let the building begin" and Annie sat transfixed. She watched a temple built; not from wood or earth or stone but from music, song and dance. Joel sang and Grace danced to Leaf's tune and as the tune climbed to crescendo and Grace spun round in Joel's song a shining temple grew around them, green and gold but full of light and colour...

When Annie woke it was way past dawn and the builders of the temple were long gone. She unwound her cramped limbs and wondered if she'd dreamed it all, but then it caught her eye-the magic Temple in the grove; of leaf and twig and flower interwoven, and still sparkling with light.

TREASURE
Inspired by 4 of Earth

Dan had always had a feeling for the land. He had roamed fields, explored forests and climbed trees as a boy; and hiked up hills and taken on the challenge of mountains in his youth. He had spent most of his life outside, living and working on the land. As he entered his later years, having discovered many of the secrets of the land and the nature of the elements, his interest had widened to the history of the land, the people and the lives they had lived. This led Dan to wander, a little slower than in his former days, with a metal detector, searching for things that had been left behind, buried in the land, like treasure, telling tales of the land and it's past. Dan was fairly lucky with his finds - instinct seemed to lead him to places where old things could be found and if he was lucky - identified or at least roughly dated.

They were only little things - scraps of metal , some of it broken pieces of jewellery that had laid there for hundreds of years, bits of ancient horse brasses Dan always got permission, for his searches. Some landowners were curious about what he found, others less interested. Some jokingly asked him if he would share the proceeds of any treasure he found, and some thought him a little crazy. It was on the land belonging to one who thought he was crazy that he ended up having the luckiest find he ever had.

It was a fine spring morning - the beginning of the metal detecting season - before the crops had really taken off and the land was pretty clear, only just coming into bud. He was wandering across a sunny field, with the detector, a field that he hadn't been in before. He had no particular thought or direction in mind but his feet, idly wandering, led him down a slight dip in the field. Suddenly the detector began to bleep. Dan swung it round slowly, in an arc, trying to pinpoint exactly where it came from. There! He had it. He put down the detector and pulled out the small digging tool he carried. He began to dig carefully. At first he could see nothing, sifting the dirt carefully through his fingers. He ran the detector over the area again and it bleeped rapidly. Sure now that he had found something, Dan began to dig in a slightly wider circle. His tool hit metal and brought to the surface not one, but a handful, of shiny gold coins. Dan's heart began to thump in his chest. He dug some more, and more coins, some falling out of a half rotted pouch of some kind, that he pulled up with the edge of his digging tool. There were loads of them- and near to the surface. Yet he could see that they were old, more than old... in fact they were ancient. Dan began to laugh out loud. He looked around him- perhaps the weather had changed the shape of the land, there had been a lot of rain- much more than usual the past winter, things could have shifted enough to bring these old coins to the top. He sat down; partly in shock- the land had yielded up treasure to him. He knew these coins would be of immense value. He picked some of them up and studied them, lying in his hand. Gleaming in the spring sun. For a moment part of him wanted to keep them for himself - to take them home and not say anything about finding them. The landowner thought Dan was a nut, so he wouldn't realise. He could find out their history by doing some research himself. But then he realised how important his discovery was - it could tell a piece of the history of his beloved land to those who came after him seeking its secrets. Not only he, but the landowner and many others could all benefit from this. Dan had no child to leave as a legacy when he died; so this would be what he left the world - a treasure of material and historical value that would outlive any child; given to him by the land he loved.

HOME IN MY POCKET
Inspired by 5 of Earth

The door slammed behind me with a loud thud and I was out in the cold; at the mercy of the elements. The wind howled and thick snowflakes whirled around me in circles. The child inside me kicked, as if angry at the cruel, cold world for refusing us shelter and warmth. My hand went automatically to stroke my swelling stomach - I would find us somewhere. I trudged through the snow, each step an effort but knowing I had to keep on, I had to survive. I had some coins, not many, but maybe enough to secure a bed for the night, in the deep pocket of the old coat I had managed to grab before I had been turfed out. I could hear them jingling as I walked. The snow began to lay on the ground and my pace slowed, I did not want to slip and fall, this child was precious to me, if to no one else, and I would make sure that he or she was never cast out and left to struggle like this. I would make a new life for the two of us. I knew not yet how or where, but determination kept my frozen feet and aching legs moving. After what seemed hours the snow seemed to lessen and the wind dropped a little and when I looked up I was able to see a light ahead of me. The child kicked again, giving me the heart to move on towards the light.

As I drew nearer I saw the inn sign swinging and stumbled towards the door, praying as I did that I could find shelter here. I pushed it open and the warmth and light from inside dazzled me momentarily, then a voice spoke to me.

"Filthy night to be out, missy"

"Yes" I said, "Have you a room? I have money." I put my hand in my pocket, fumbling for the coins, but there was nothing there, nothing but a hole in my pocket! My knees buckled and what little strength I had drained from my body. I felt hands lifting me and soft words being murmured as I was eased into a chair near the fire. A cup was put to my lips and I sipped obediently, feeling the liquid warm me as I swallowed it.

"Never mind what you have, or don't have, I'd not see a dog out on a night like this" said the voice. Relief flooded through me, this night at least my child and I would survive, and tomorrow was another day.

THE PEDLAR
Inspired by 6 of Earth

I ran down the path and through the garden gate after the pedlar before anyone could stop me, clutching the little pouch he had dropped on our garden path.

"Excuse me.." I called, as I spotted him up ahead. He stopped and turned round. He smiled when he saw me.

"Did you want something, Missy?" he said, regarding me with twinkling eyes that shone in a nut brown face.

I smiled back and showed him the pouch he had dropped.

"I came to give you this back, you dropped it." I said. He looked down at it and then back at my face, studying me for several long moments.

"Keep it "he said, at last." It might be just what you need". With that he turned and walked away.

"But I ..." I stammered in confusion to his fast retreating back, then he took the forest path and disappeared from view. What a strange thing he had said, I thought to myself. How could he know what I might need? He didn't know me.... did he? I weighed the pouch in my hand, trying to guess what it contained. It felt like stones- I shook it and felt them rattle together. Why would he give me a bag of stones? Curiosity triumphed over confusion and I decided the only way to find out was to open the pouch and tip out the contents. So I sat down and tipped it out on the grass. At first I thought they were just stones or pebbles, but as I looked closer I saw that they all had markings on them, different markings on each one. I laid them out and counted them, there were twenty four with marks on and one blank one. I held the blank one in my hand and instantly I knew what it meant. Amazed and wondering what was happening, I put it down and picked up another. I stared at it, tracing its mark with my thumb. I felt a stirring feeling, like the wind rising. Certain now that it was time to take my gift and go, I gathered up the rest of the stones and turned back towards home and the privacy of my room, with the pouch nestled safely in my pocket.

It took me many years to learn to use the gift the pedlar gave me according to its true purpose, and to share its many benefits with those around me. I never saw him again, though I often pictured his face in my mind, but eventually I came to understand the wisdom of his words- for it was indeed, just what I needed.

SEVEN MILE LANE
Inspired by 7 of Earth

Last night I dreamt of walking along Seven Mile Lane. It was twilight in my dream, a strange time to set out on a journey, yet I knew that it was right. The trees either side of the road cast shadows but I felt no fear, only the certainty that I must walk the seven miles to the end. I set off at a steady pace, whistling to keep myself cheerful and looking up at the sky above, hoping to spot the first star to come out so I could wish on it. What did I want from my life? What would I wish for? I asked myself as I walked. Not riches, money made no one happy. Not fame, fame was no guarantee of happiness either, nor was power.

If anything I would wish to grow and bloom, move on and progress and to know how to achieve this. Could I wish for all this on just one star? Maybe, maybe not. Maybe I should just wish to reach my destination at the end of Seven Mile Lane. As my dreaming self thought that thought, the first star appeared, glimmering through the trees and shining a soft beam of light on the road I trod - as if to say yes, this is the thing to wish for now, and this is the purpose of the star; to guide me safely past the wildness that dwelt in the woods that edged the road, the as yet unseen obstacles that may be strewn in my path.

Comforted, I fixed my eyes on the star and my feet fell into a sure and steady rhythm, I knew that I must keep on going. On and on I walked, still fixed on that star, and did not tire at all. I knew that something right and good waited for me at the end of the road, that the purpose of my journey would be revealed, so each step took me nearer and nearer. The moon rose and hung in the sky, like a magical lamp, lighting my way. I heard an owl hoot in the distance and still I plodded on, on and on until the road ended. The seven miles were behind me at last and before me I saw a field of golden flowers, my heart lifted and I woke knowing that my wishes would be granted.

WOODY
Inspired by 8 of Earth

Of all the apprentices I had there was one I would never forget. Woody was what everyone called him, and we never knew if he had another name. He had just turned up out of the forest one day, a scruffy country boy, and knocked at my door. He said he had seen the furniture I made from wood and he would like to learn to make fine pieces. He asked if I would teach him how, and let him work for me in return. He wasn't worried about wages; bed and board would do him. I could always use another set of muscles so I took him on. He was strange lad; he didn't talk much or mess about with the other lads. His focus was entirely on what he wanted to learn. He followed my every move, to begin with. He even got up at the crack of dawn to follow me into the forest to choose the wood we would use, while his fellows lay in their beds. As we walked amongst the trees he would stand and gaze at them, from root to topmost branch. He would ask their names and their qualities and sometimes he would reach out and touch them, or sit beneath them, as if absorbing something from them. He treated them with the utmost respect, almost as if they were sacred.

The other lads soon marked him out as odd and called him 'forest boy', not that he took any notice. He just worked away steadily. At first his efforts at furniture making were rough, but he applied himself with enthusiasm and quickly mastered the basics.

I came upon him late one night, as he began to progress to decorative work, carving an intricate pattern upon a small but very elegant chair he had made. I felt a thrill of excitement; it was clear that that Woody had a special talent. This lad was an artist- he had a feel for the nature of the wood. From the strange and silent communion he had had with the growing tree, he had somehow captured its essence and brought it out in his carving. His long fingered hands had shaped with wood with love and released its beauty.

After a spell he looked up and saw me watching him.

"That's beautiful, Woody" I said" That'll sell for a good price"

He smiled a rare smile at me; "Money has its uses, master, but I would do this for love" he said.

That was many years ago now and Woody is long gone. It had not taken long for him to learn all of my skills and perform them better than I did and I knew he had to go. Woody needed to take his gift out to the wider world. We parted fondly, but I was sorry to see him leave, for as I had taught him, I had also learned from him. He reminded me of things I had long forgotten, when he connected with the spirit of the trees and expressed it in his work. And after he left I did my best to teach other lads to work the way he did. None of them ever got to be quite like Woody, I never saw that magic touch again, but we all did well from it. Many of my lads went on to make fine furniture for the town and forest folk.

PATIENCE
Inspired by 9 of Earth

Nine times the moon had waxed and waned since Patience had begun herself appointed task. Rocking herself gently to and fro on the old swing she thought back to how the garden was when she first saw it- wild and overgrown, with weeds choking the flowerbeds and camouflaging the paths. It had been the smell of honeysuckle after a shower of rain that had drawn her there in the first place- enticing her in as if asking to be freed from the stranglehold of the weeds. The wind had seemed to whisper to her as it wound restlessly round the trees at the end of the garden that were half buried in long grass and smothered with ivy.

She hadn't been sure of what she was doing to begin with, but she had learned as she went along. Slowly and steadily Patience had worked; she had weeded and pruned. She had dug over the rich black soil, burying deep, with her bare hands, the tiny seeds she had gathered to plant. On and on, through rain and shine, she had worked, watering and nurturing and caring for the budding plants. She found herself changing as the garden changed. She grew leaner and fitter from the physical labour as the shape of the garden began to reveal itself. She found a feeling of peace and contentment as she worked in solitude that grew as slowly and silently as the seeds.

Her skin glowed with colour and life as she, like her flowers, turned to face the sun. And as the fruits ripened on the branches in the garden Patience came to some conclusions about herself and her life. She knew for sure and certain now who she was and where she was going.

Jumping off the swing and gathering her tools she took one last look around the garden. There was a sold sign at the front of the house, the new owners would soon be moving in. Patience smiled to herself, she hoped the garden would work its magic for them too.

FOREST HOME
Inspired by 10 of Earth

I left home when I was just sixteen - the old traditional Forest ways were too much for me, too stifling. It wasn't the place - I loved the place, still do, it's in my blood I suppose. It was the people, the old people mainly, with their rules and regulations, that entangled me and made me feel trapped, made me run away to seek my fortune in the big wide world. But I always knew I would come back to the place of my ancestors where my roots were - but years and years later, when most of those old people were gone and no one would remember me.

And so it happened. At first it seemed by chance I saw a painting in a gallery in the far off city I lived in - of bluebells, reminding me of those that grew at home. Then, again by chance, a tree fell into the building I lived in after a storm, causing structural damage, and I was forced to begin looking for a new home. I thought my luck was really running out when, by chance once more, a surprise inheritance from a long forgotten great uncle enabled me to approach an estate agent.

The size of my inheritance made a wide range of properties available to me; you could say I was spoilt for choice.

"Have you any idea what you actually want? Or even where? "Asked the exasperated estate agent.

"I want somewhere to settle - somewhere in the country - you know trees, fields…., anywhere like that…" I said - more for something to say really, not because I knew what I wanted - I didn't - or I thought I didn't.

He shuffled his papers, mumbling to himself.

"Ahh, here they are." With a flourish he placed three photographs on the table. And then it happened - one of those rare magic moments in life - I looked straight at the photo in the centre of a house on the edge of a forest, surrounded by bluebells. I picked it up.

"This is it, this is the one" I said, handing it to him

"Ah yes, lovely location, way out in the country, just on the edge of the Forest, needs a little work done on it though..."

"No problem, I'll do it" I said

And so it became mine - the old house on the Forest edge that I used to come to when I was a child. Something about it had always stopped me in my tracks. I used to peer over the gate, trying to see in the windows. The garden behind merged with the Forest so you were never sure where the garden ended and Forest began.

The bluebells were in bloom when I moved in, their tiny heads bobbing a greeting as I stepped through the gate at last. A deep contentment filled me and I stood there savouring the moment. The smell of the Forest filled my nose - the rich greens of the trees filled my eyes. I was in no hurry to go inside so I wandered round the side of the house to the garden at the back. It was full of plants and flowers, in beautiful abundance as if laid out in a celebration of its richness for me.

I carried on exploring it and at last I came to the crowning glory, at the far end of the garden - ten full grown apple trees, in glorious bloom, growing in a circle, like a magical Druids Grove. As I walked amongst them, I knew that I was truly home.

CRAB APPLE
Inspired by Page of Earth

"You are supposed to ask first" said a voice as I reached out to pick one of the hard little crab apples from the low, twisty, branch. I looked up to see a fierce little face peering at me through the leaves.

"This is a sacred tree" it said proudly," One of the seven chieftain trees of Britain in fact"

"Does it belong to you?" I asked politely, not daring now to pick the fruit.

"It doesn't belong to me" came the scornful answer "I belong to it. I am the Resident in this crab apple"

The creature stepped forth from the tree and stood before me. He was rather like the tree in appearance; small and sturdy and dressed in green, with rosy pink cheeks and a wreath of mistletoe on his head.

"I am the Guardian of this tree" he finished, puffing out his chest importantly. "You have to approach me first if you wish to eat of this tree's fruit"

"I see" I said, although I was not sure that I did, this had never happened to me before.

"This may not have happened to you before" he said, " But this is a special time, the Elder Mother of all the Forest has decreed that we shall all offer our fruits to your kind, but just for three days, we don't want the trees all stripped bare."

"And if I eat the fruit at this special time?" I asked I had a vague memory of a warning about eating food offered by otherworldly creatures.

"You were going to pick it anyway" he reminded me.

"Yes, but I..." I stammered

"You'll come to no harm, fool," he said, crossly, "This tree's fruit will heal your ills and open our heart. But first you must ask, and if you want to really do it properly you will make an offering to the tree in return for the sacred fruit of knowledge. That ribbon in your hair will do nicely. Now, say after me..."

I carefully repeated the words he said (words that alas, I can no longer remember) and pulled the ribbon from my hair. Silently he motioned me to pick an apple and eat it. I closed my eyes as the tart fruit woke my taste buds to a delight I never thought possible.

When I opened my eyes the Guardian was gone, but the fruit was not, so I ate every bit of it- pips and all.

WARRIORS
Inspired by Knight of Earth

There was a monument in one of Farmer Neath's fields. Some Stone Age thing, they had told Johnny. Two tall stones with one on top, like a roof. They said it was a monument to an ancient warrior, but then Johnny didn't know much about warriors, he only knew about farm work.

The weather changed on the first day of the harvest. Just as Johnny stopped for lunch the heavens opened. Grabbing his sandwich box he ran to the only place of shelter he could see; the monument. Johnny squatted under the low roof and leaned against one of the side pillars, contentedly munching his sandwiches. The rain poured steadily down so Johnny sat where he was, no good trying to work in this, he thought.

Within minutes the drumming of the rain on the stone roof had lulled him to a deep relaxation. As his eyes gradually closed he fell into another world, another time......

Warriors, clad in fur and skin with huge spears, milled about the field. There was smell of burning and hoarse, angry cries in some guttural language filled the smoky air. Johnny was crouching behind a chariot, looking down at himself, he saw, not the familiar work jeans, but clothes of skin and fur. In his clenched fist was a short spear, from his belt hung a blunt club. His heart skipped a beat. What was going on? Where was he? Cautiously, he edged round the chariot to try and see what was around him. The field sloped downwards slightly and below where he crouched small skirmishes were going on. Big hairy men lumbered towards each other roaring, while others got entangled in the melee around them. Then Johnny heard shouting and the skirmishes stopped, suddenly. A respectful hush filled the air as six huge men came through the crowds carrying a dead warrior up the hill. Johnny looked behind him and above where he was he saw more men levering two huge stones into place while others joined to lift a third to roof the structure. To the beat of an unseen drum he watched the dead hero being carried to his resting place. When the bearers reached their destination silence fell again and Johnny knew where he was. But how would he get back? How had he even got here in the first place? Following his instinct he made his way to the stones, unnoticed in the crowd, and as he walked past the fallen warrior with his head bowed, paying his respects as deeply and truly as the others did, although he didn't know why or how, he stepped back to the world he had left.

The field was deserted and the rain still fell, no more harvest work was done that day, but Johnny knew about warriors now and about respect.

THE WOMAN WHO PLANTED A TREE
Inspired by Queen of Earth

The Trees whispered among themselves as the Sun rose that morning, "The Queen is coming, the Queen is coming". The breeze carried the message from Birch to Alder, from Hawthorn to Ash. By noon the whole Forest knew that the Queen was coming to plant a new Tree to give thanks for the safe birth of her new born child. The woodland creatures and other Forest folk gathered together all the fruits the Forest could offer for this time of celebration: nuts and berries, juicy apples and crisp pears. The flowering Gorse and Heather decked the glade with glorious colour and the Stream that ran through the Forest offered sparkling wine to drink. At last her leather booted feet stepped on the stone path that led to the open Forest Gate and then she was there, in the glade. A hush fell as she stepped forward. She threw off her warm cloak and pulled up the sleeves of her green velvet gown. She knelt before a bare patch of fertile Forest soil and, putting the tiny Tree she carried to one side, she began to dig with her hands. Soft white hands with gold rings and jeweled bracelets dug into the rich black earth, her thick brown hair fell forward covering her face as she worked. When the hole was deep enough she carefully placed the tiny Tree in it and repacked the displaced earth around it.

In one graceful movement she stood and opened her arms. The Forest dwellers sank to their knees, entranced by her beauty. Her cheeks glowed pink and her red lips parted in a smile.

"As the life of this Tree begins with the life of the Kingdom's heir both I will tend with love both shall be in my care"

Taking a phial of liquid from the belt at her slim waist, she poured it over the little Tree. As she poured the glittering droplets, tiny buds peeped through on the miniscule branches.

"As this Tree grows tall spreads from Earth to Sky both shall thrive be great, strong and wise"

Turning away from the Tree to face the Forest folk she spoke again; "Make Sacred this Tree, see it comes to no harm for to do such a thing could destroy the charm

The life of this Tree is forever bound with the child who one day will rule your land."

Her arms dropped to her sides and she smiled round at them. "Now rise up my friends and celebrate!"

As one, the Forest folk leapt to their feet and the celebration began...

Much later a woman in a brown coat and a green dress slipped quietly back through the Forest Gate, her muddy hands thrust in her pockets and a satisfied smile on her face. Unnoticed by anyone, she returned to her ordinary life.
Green Eyes
Inspired by King of Earth

The swollen black cloud burst over the green field and cursing, I ran towards the hillside for cover. Stepping through two large stones, half buried in the ground, I found the entrance to a cave and huddled gratefully within the opening, wondering how long the rain would last.

"Quite a while, I should think" said a voice behind me, answering my unspoken question.

Startled, I turned and peered into the gloom behind me. As thunder rumbled outside, a tall dark man rose from a squatting position and stepped towards me. His features were unclear in the poor light, but his green eyes glittered and a flash of lightening illuminated his white teeth and outlined his powerful frame against the background of the cave.

"I did not mean to startle you" he said" I was about to prepare a meal. It would be nice to have some human company while the storm rages."

"Thanks "I said. This unexpected invitation was at least preferable to braving the storm outside. Tentatively, I moved away from the cave's entrance.

"Can I help?" I asked. The green eyes glittered again as he passed me a small cooking pot half filled with fragrant herbs.

"You can put this outside to catch us some rainwater while I light the fire"

Pushing up my sleeve to avoid getting soaked, I thrust the cooking point outside and watched as it quickly filled with rainwater. When I turned to give it to him he had a merry blaze already burning.

"That was quick" I said. He smiled at me and sat back on his haunches.

"It doesn't take long when you know how" he said. "Come and sit while the food cooks and tell me of yourself".

So I sat and told him of myself and my life in the village over the hill and he listened, nodding occasionally and stirring the pot. Then he told me a little of his life; roaming the hills and valleys of the land ,having mostly animals for companions, finding shelter in forests and caves and living on what the land offered him.

As we shared the delicious soup he had made I asked him why he chose to live this way. He smiled and touched my hand; something seemed to flare between us

"Because my only concerns are putting food in my belly and finding some place to rest. This way the whole land is my kingdom." I smiled back at him, what he said made perfect sense. Drowsy with fullness I leaned back against the cave wall and must have fallen asleep. When I woke the storm was passed and the cave, silent and empty. I went outside hoping to find him there, but he had gone, so a little sadly I set off to walk home. I had not gone far when I heard a loud bellowing. I stopped and turned back and there on top of the hill stood a magnificent stag with huge antlers. Green eyes glittered at me again and a life changing understanding coursed through me as I raised my hand in farewell.

THE END

It has taken me several years to complete my journey through the Tarot whilst combining it with Story. As I travelled this long and winding road I made many discoveries. One of the first things I learned was that the major cards told a very different kind of tale to the minor cards. The archetypal qualities of the major cards came through very clearly and I found, surprisingly, that these stories were not difficult to write; in fact it almost seemed as if they were being dictated to me. They seemed to have a very magical feel to them and I felt myself experiencing each tale as it unfolded, this may be the reason that these stories are all written in the first person. The minor stories, although they were also magical, felt quite different and many more of them related to the everyday world that we all know and to the events and feelings that we all experience.

Combining cards to make stories was yet another kind of adventure, teaching me much more about how the cards could relate to each other and how these combinations very often reflected real life situations. So I learned not only about the individual energies of the cards, but how they related to each other and how these interactions related to happenings in real people's lives.

Stories written by others played a great part in this work as well, illustrating and illuminating aspects of the Tarot to me and those around me, as did many ancient myths, legends and fairy tales.

This journey taught me much about the different uses of Tarot and Story; particularly the therapeutic and creative uses of both. My clients gained as many benefits from this exploration as I did, and may I say here how grateful I am to those who accompanied me on parts of my journey, which clearly proved that this study was not merely an academic exercise, but was of practical use to anyone who chose to avail themselves of it.

It was quite difficult to come to the end of this journey and it is quite likely that I will revisit some of its many stages in the future. I do not doubt there are always more stories to be written with different combinations of cards. But my final conclusion (for now!) is that no matter what your story- the Tarot will tell it!

EPILOGUE

TABLE OF CORRESPONDENCES

This table is made up of many kinds of stories and characters from stories who I felt embodied the energies that are shown by the cards. Fables, myths, legends, faery tales, classic and contempory stories are all included. Some are short stories, some are whole books and some are particular characters from books or stories. My sources were not one , but many Tarot packs, and the considerable amount of books on my shelves at the time of writing, and many of the stories I have read or been told in the past. I also discovered and enjoyed lots of new stories on my search to link tales to Tarot cards.

I have included the authors in the list except in the case of the myths, legends and faery tales. Some of the cards have several attributions and this list could actually go on forever, I noticed this when trying to choose attributions to the Fool card- almost every hero or heroine of every story could have been a Fool. And of course, other readers could link entirely different stories and characters to the cards.

Overall this task turned out to be easier than I had expected it to be. Mostly this was due to the wealth of material available. The world is full of stories and at times I was spoilt for choice. I linked the major cards with stories relatively quickly. I attributed this to the fact that many stories have archetypal themes that relate naturally to those represented by the major cards. The Lovers was one of the cards that required the least research as this is one of the most popular themes. I found that the minor cards took more thought and more research in order to check out my initial ideas. Sometimes my idea began with a title- an example of this was The Moonstone by Wilkie Collins, attributed in the list to the Ace of earth. I had not read this story, but seeing as it was about a jewel and that the ace can relate to a material possession such as this, I thought it was worth reading to see if it linked to the ace of earth in any other way. The underlying theme of the book was the search for the real truth, which convinced me of its suitability, as finding a truth in the real world is often an issue raised by this card. Another story whose title drew me was Forrest Carter's The Education of Little Tree, as study is so often related to the page of earth and trees are ideal representatives of this suit, this title - and the story of how what Little Tree's Cherokee grandparents taught him transformed his life, was very apt for this transformative card. But it was not the title that led me to link the Justice card with To Kill a Mockingbird by Harper Lee, the content of the story-Atticus Finch's dedication to rightness and the theme of justice for Tom Robinson-clearly demonstrated the energy of the card.

There were some cards I became temporarily 'stuck on' and some were more difficult to find stories for than others, but I feel that these were the cards I needed to work with the most, and part of the task was a deepening of my own understanding of those cards.

I learned from this that the Tarot was even more flexible than I had thought it to be. I also noticed that the Tarot related to the stories much more than I had expected it to. The possibility of an infinite supply of stories and interpretations helped me to identify much wider ranging interpretations of each card.

MAJOR CARDS

Fool
Dorothy from the Wizard of Oz, Peter Pan by J.M. Barrie, Mowgli from Jungle Book by Rudyard Kipling, Harry Potter by J. K Rowling.

Magician
The Book of Merlin by T H White, Millroy the Magician by Paul Theroux

High Priestess
Mary Poppins by P. L. Travers, Legend of The Lady of the Lake (Arthurian), Tinkerbell from Peter Pan by J. M Barrie, Morgain from Mists of Avalon by Marion Zimmer Bradley
Moonheart by Charles de Lint

Empress
The Guinevere Trilogy by Rosalind Miles, Fancy Deverell from Paint the Wind by Cathy Cash Spellman, Wendy from Peter Pan by J M Barrie, Ma Larkin from The Darling Buds of May by H.E. Bates

Emperor
Arthur by Stephen Lawhead - Don Corleone from The Godfather by Mario Puzo

Hierophant
Taliesin by Stephen Lawhead, Ralph de Bricassart from The Thorn Birds by Colleen McCoulough

Lovers
Romeo and Juliet by William Shakespeare, Legend of Tristan and Isolde (Celtic), Hansel and Gretel, The Weasely Twins from the Harry Potter books by J.K.Rowling

Chariot
The Pilgrimage by Paul Coelho, Legend of the Quest for the Holy Grail (Arthurian), The Wizard of Oz
The Unlikely Ones by Mary Brown, The Celestine Prophecy by James Redman

Strength
The Horse Whisperer by Nicholas Evans, Beauty and the Beast, Call of the Wild by Jack London

Hermit
Legend of the Grail Hermit (Arthurian) Max de Winter from Rebecca by Daphne du Maurier, Morda from the Legend of Little Gwion, (Celtic)

Wheel of Fortune
Legend of the Round Table (Arthurian), The Wheel of Fortune by Susan Howatch, Legend of the Spinners of Fate (Celtic)

Justice
The Merchant of Venice by William Shakespeare, To Kill a Mockingbird by Harper Lee

Hanged Man
Sophie's Choice, by William Styron, Dances with Wolves by Michael Blake

Death
Sleeping Beauty, White Raven by Diana Paxon

Temperance
The Rainbow Path by Stephanie Wilson, The Last Rainbow by Parke Godwin
The Legend of Iris (Greek)

Devil
The Witches of Eastwick by John Updike, Red Riding Hood. The Trickster by Muriel Gray, Rumpelstiltskin, Ceremonies by T.E.D.Klein

Tower
Rapunzel, Wuthering Heights by Charlotte Bronte

Star
A Midsummer Night's Dream by William Shakespeare, a Trip to the Stars- by Nicholas Christopher

Sun
Legend of Appollo (Greek). Legend of Lugh of the Long Hand (Celtic)

Moon
Cinderella, Alice in Wonderland by Lewis Carrol, Memory and Dream by Charles de Lint

Judgment
Legend of the Sleeping Lord (Arthurian), The Ugly Duckling

World
Centennial and Hawaii- by James A Mitchener, Forest by Edward Rutherford, Jungle Book by Rudyard Kipling

MINOR CARDS

EARTH CARDS

Ace- The Moonstone by Wilkie Collins
2- The Angler and the Little Fish from Aesop's Fables
3- The Homespun Tunic (Arthurian Legend)
4- Shylock from the Merchant of Venice by William Shakespeare
5- Katie Mulholland by Catherine Cookson
6- Eriu, Banba and Fodhla (Irish legend)
7- The Seven Dwarves
8- The Sorcerer's Apprentice
9- Into the Green by Charles de Lint
10- Treasure Island by Robert Louis Stevenson, The Legend of Camelot (Arthurian)
Page- The Education of Little Tree by Forest Carter
Knight- The Legend of Johnny Appleseed, (American)
Queen- Rose by Martin Cruz Smith
King- Pa Larkin- from The Darling Buds of May by H.E Bates,

WATER CARDS

Ace- The Magic Cup by A. M. Greeley, Legend of the Holy Grail (Arthurian)
2- Oisin and Niamh (Celtic myth)
3- The Dream of Oengus (Celtic myth)
4- The Wooing of Etain (Celtic myth)
5- The Great Hag who fell Asleep (Celtic myth)
6- The Water Babies by Kingsley Amis
7- Legend of Thomas the Rhymer (Scottish), Abel, Baker, Charlie by John Maxim

8- The Voyage of Mael Duinn (Celtic myth)
9- The Contest of Jupiter from Aesop's fables
10 The Prince and the Pilgrim by Mary Stewart
Page-Winnie the Pooh by A. A. Milne,
Knight- Sir Galahad (Grail legend)
Queen- Sea Priestess by Dion Fortune
King-Legend of the Fisher King (Celtic), Captain Correlli from Captain Corelli's Mandolin by Louis

AIR CARDS

Ace- Excalibur (Arthurian legend)
2-The Crow Sisters by Charles de Lint
3- Aoife and Cu Chulainn (Celtic myth)
4-Airmed- daughter of Diancecht (Irish myth)
5-Jessica by Bryce Courtney
6 -The Six Swan Brothers from the Daughter of the Forest trilogy by Juliet de Marillier
7 - Papillon by Henri Charriere
8 -Sionnan (Celtic myth)
9- Macbeth by William Shakespeare, Insomnia by Steven King
10- At the back of the North Wind by George Macdonald,
Page- Nancy from Oliver Twist by Charles Dickens
Knight- Robin Hood (English legend), James Bond by Ian Fleming
Queen - Miss Marple by Agatha Christie, Miss Havisham from Great Expectations by Charles Dickens
King- Inspector Morse by Colin Dexter, Hercule Poirot by Agatha Christie

FIRE CARDS

Ace- Bolga's Spear (Celtic myth)
2 The Eagle and the Crow- from Aesops fables

3- Jamaica Inn by Daphne du Maurier
4- The Way of Wyrd by Brian Bates
5- The Last Companion by Patrick Mc Cormack
6- Firelord by Parke Godwin
7- The Enclosure of the Seven Doors (Celtic myth)
8- The White Hart (Arthurian Legend)
9- The Iron Lance by Stephen Lawhead
10- The Firebrand by Marion Zimmer Bradley
Page- The Dragon Queen by Alice Borchardt
Knight- The Pied Piper of Hamelin
Queen- Scarlett O hara from Gone with the Wind by Margaret Mitchell
King- The Smoke Jumper by Nicholas Evans, The Fire Bringer by D. Clement Davis

BIOGRAPHY

Fairy Tales and Therapy	Dick Leith
The Dreaming of Place	Hugh Lampton
Encyclopedia of Myths and Legends of the British Isle	Various
Tarot Therapy	Steve Hounsome
The Myth of the Goddess	Anne Baring and Jules Cashford
Forest of Souls	Rachel Pollack
Ancient Irish Legend	Padriac O'Farrell
Celtic Bards, Celtic Druid	R.J.Stewart and Robin Williams
Encyclopedia of Arthurian Legends	Ronan Coghlan
The Mythic Tarot Workbook	Juliet Sharman-Burke
The Inner Child Tarot	Isha and Mark Lerner
The Larousse Encyclopedia of Mythology	Various
The Shakespeare Tarot	Dolores Ashcroft-Nowicki
The Arthurian Tarot	John and Caitlin Matthews
Hallowquest	John and Caitlin Matthews
The Celtic Wisdom Tarot	Caitlin Matthews
A Fairy Tale Reader	John and Caitlin Matthews
The Complete Tales of the Brothers Grimm	Brothers Grimm
The Complete Works of William Shakespeare	William Shakespeare
The Chronicles of Narnia	C.S. Lewis
Just So Stories	Rudyard Kipling
A Guide to Occult Britain	John Wilcock
The Lore of the Forest	Alexander Porteous
Field Guide to the Little People	Nancy Arrowsmith George Moorse
The Writers Journey	Christopher Vogler
Hero with a Thousand faces	Joseph Cambell
Tarot Shadow Work	Christine Jette
Tarot and Dream Interpretation	Julie Gillentine
The Silver Branch Cards	Nicholas R. Mann
Wuthering Heights	Emily Bronte

The Education of Little Tree   Forest Carter
Rebecca   Daphne du Maurier
Mary Poppins   P.L. Travers

Printed in Great Britain
by Amazon